THROUGH THE
FRENCH
CANALS

Other titles of interest

Cruising French Waterways 2nd edition
Hugh McKnight
ISBN 0–7136–3282–8
This fully comprehensive guide to the varied network of French
inland waterways gives the histories of the navigations, together
with details of *châteaux* and other interesting buildings, historic
sites and local attractions, making it ideal for holiday cruising.
It also provides practical information on moorings, repair yards,
shops, restaurants, fuel and water points and other facilities.

Through the Dutch and Belgian Canals 8th edition
Philip Bristow
ISBN 0–7136–5760–X
This invaluable guide describes 39 Dutch and 20 Belgian routes,
pointing out the many sights and places of interest along the way.
The author provides a wealth of practical advice on cruise
planning, the suitability of different boats, canal signals and
'rules of the road'.

Through the German Waterways
Philip Bristow
ISBN 0–7136–5770–7
24 routes are described and illustrated, and information given on
the Rhine–Maine–Danube link. The author offers advice on
choosing a suitable boat and planning cruises as well as providing
information on the cost of living in West Germany.

Slow Boat Through Germany
Hugh McKnight
ISBN 0–7136–3778–1
This book will tempt all adventurous inland boaters to wander
into the heart of Europe. Hugh McKnight demonstrates that the
German network is a fascinating web of watery highways awaiting
discovery. He tells of his own cruises in the region and gives all
the necessary planning detail to explore the country's most
appealing and interesting navigations.

The Inland Waterways Manual A complete guide to boating on
rivers, lakes and canals
Emrhys Barrell
ISBN 0–7136–3693–9
A complete guide for newcomers to boating on the inland
waterways and the only book anyone will ever need to buy to take
their first steps afloat.

THROUGH THE FRENCH CANALS

Philip Bristow

Eighth edition

Adlard Coles Nautical
London

This edition published in 1994 by Adlard Coles Nautical
an imprint of A & C Black (Publishers) Ltd
35 Bedford Row, London WC1R 4JH

First edition published by Navigator Books 1970
Second edition Nautical Books 1972
Third edition Nautical Books 1975
Fourth edition Nautical Books 1979
Fifth edition Nautical Books 1982
Sixth edition Nautical Books 1987
Seventh edition Nautical Books 1990
Eighth edition Adlard Coles Nautical 1994

ISBN 0-7136-3844-3

A CIP catalogue record for this book is
available from the British Library

Typeset in Monophoto 10½ on 12pt Goudy Old Style
by August Filmsetting, Haydock, St Helens
Printed and bound in Great Britain by The Cromwell
Press, Melksham, Wiltshire

*Despite every effort to ensure that information given in this
book is accurate and up to date, it is regretted that neither author
nor publisher can accept responsibility for errors or omissions.*

To Emma
perfect companion of many cruises who made this book possible

Acknowledgements

I am indebted to many Departments of the French Government for the facts and figures that they have kindly made available to me; to the many offices of the *Syndicat d'Initiative* who have patiently dealt with my considerable demands upon their time; and particularly to Georges Normand, *Chargé de Mission, Commissariat Général au Tourisme*, 8 avenue de l'Opera, Paris, for his kindness and help.

Note: Depths of water are shown throughout in metres, including all harbour plans.

Contents

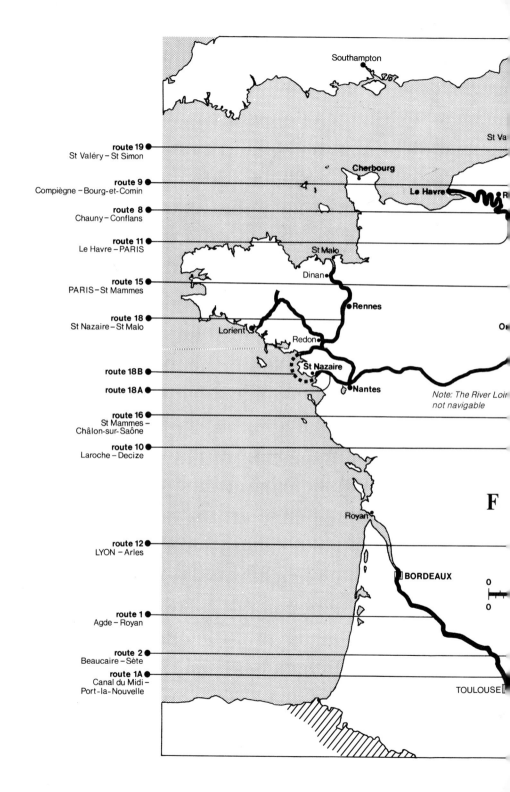

Southampton

St Va

route 19 ●
St Valéry – St Simon

route 9 ●
Compiègne – Bourg-et-Comin

Cherbourg

Le Havre

R

route 8 ●
Chauny – Conflans

route 11 ●
Le Havre – PARIS

St Malo

Dinan ●

route 15 ●
PARIS – St Mammes

route 18 ●
St Nazaire – St Malo

● Rennes

Lorient

Redon ●

O

route 18 B ●

St Nazaire

route 18 A ●

● Nantes

Note: The River Loir
not navigable

route 16 ●
St Mammes –
Châlon-sur-Saône

route 10 ●
Laroche – Decize

F

Royan ●

route 12 ●
LYON – Arles

▮ **BORDEAUX**

0

route 1 ●
Agde – Royan

0

route 2 ●
Beaucaire – Sète

route 1A ●
Canal du Midi –
Port-la-Nouvelle

TOULOUSE ▮

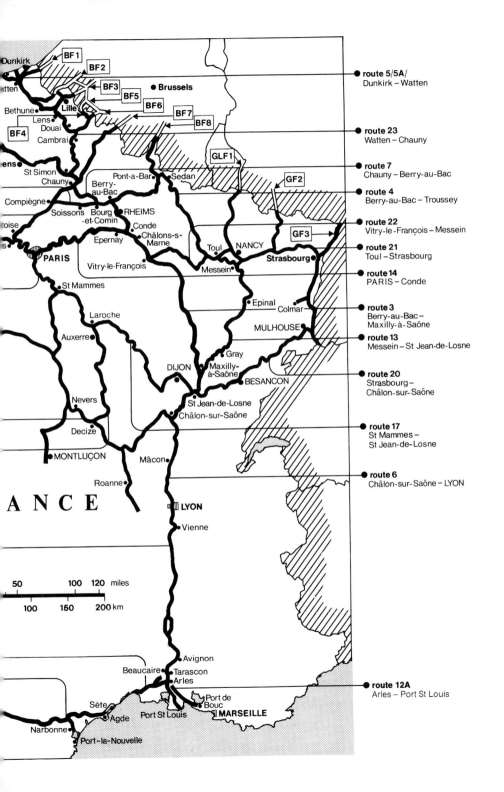

Dunkirk

BF 1

BF 2

BF 3 Brussels

BF 5

BF 6

Bethune

Lens Lille BF 7

Douai BF 8

BF 4 Cambrai

St Simon

Chauny Pont-a-Bar Sedan

Berry- GLF 1

au-Bac

Compiègne Soissons Bourg RHEIMS GF 2

-et-Comin Conde

Châlons-s-

Epernay Marne

Toul NANCY

PARIS Vitry-le-François GF 3

Messein Strasbourg

St Mammes

Epinal Colmar

Laroche MULHOUSE

Auxerre

Gray

DIJON Maxilly-

à-Saône

Nevers BESANCON

St Jean-de-Losne

Decize Châlon-sur-Saône

MONTLUÇON Mâcon

Roanne

A N C E

LYON

Vienne

50 100 120 miles

100 150 200 km

Avignon

Beaucaire Tarascon

Arles

Sète Port de

Agde Bouc

Port St Louis MARSEILLE

Narbonne

Port-la-Nouvelle

● route 5/5A/
Dunkirk – Watten

● route 23
Watten – Chauny

● route 7
Chauny – Berry-au-Bac

● route 4
Berry-au-Bac – Troussey

● route 22
Vitry-le-François – Messein

● route 21
Toul – Strasbourg

● route 14
PARIS – Conde

● route 3
Berry-au-Bac –
Maxilly-à-Saône

● route 13
Messein – St Jean-de-Losne

● route 20
Strasbourg –
Châlon-sur-Saône

● route 17
St Mammes –
St Jean-de-Losne

● route 6
Châlon-sur-Saône – LYON

● route 12A
Arles – Port St Louis

Berry au Bac. Canal latéral à l'Aisne. Barge with wheelhouse folded down.

Introduction

by Georges Normand, Chargé de Mission
Commissariat Général au Tourisme
8 avenue de l'Opéra, Paris

How to travel in France

I am pleased to have this opportunity to write the introduction
to Philip Bristow's book because of my recent interest in the
rivers and canals of France. I discovered that our waterways
were by far the most beautiful in Europe and was surprised to
find that one could travel around almost all of France by boat.

I also found that other countries were utilizing waterways for
tourism in a way we were not; so I want to enthusiastically
recommend them as another way of enjoying one's vacation.

Water-roads

Waterways are off the beaten track, away from the noise of
highways, away from the multiple dangers of high-speed
driving, away from polluted air, crowds, another world so
different from ours that once you have tried waterway cruising,
your conception of leisure, your dreams of future vacations will
be changed. Enjoy the luxury of quiet days with a speed limit of
5 knots on peaceful canals where you will find peace and repose
for the body and soul. A therapeutic treatment like a spa, only
you will float on the water, not drink it.

How does one 'travel' on these waterways? By boat, of
course. Not so much 'travel', but float, glide, or paddle the
canals. On board you can have a bicycle to ride the canal roads;
camping equipment, so that you can find a wild bank, pitch a
tent and stay longer. This is an inexpensive and a liberated way
to move about. No policeman will stop you for speeding.

If you are more mechanically inclined, you can always take a
small boat with an outboard motor, follow the same waterways;
you will be asked for nothing or charged nothing as you stop
over. On your way you will find some lovely little auberges,
where you can have a drink or a good meal, *pas cher*.

You may prefer a more elaborate way of travelling. Any boat, whose draft is around 1.22 m (with an air draft of 3.05 m), will carry you all over France (length 35.35 m, width 4.72 m). You should check your route, as some of the waterways have locks shorter than those dimensions. Some French boat builders have realized, following the example of the United States, that the houseboat is the most convenient on the waterways.

Some captains prefer to be at the wheel of a 'he' boat, one that looks like one. But often, the lady partner of a boat prefers to have a 'she' boat – one with comforts such as a fridge, gas oven, shower, and what not. I like comfort myself, and think that houseboats are the most comfortable means to explore the waterways.

If you don't want the responsibility of driving your own boat, one you either own or rent, you can use cruise boats or hotel boats, a most enjoyable way of visiting a country like France. There are charter boats offering full comfort, fine food, good accommodation, plus excursions along the way. The water-roads of France are lovely, restful, and often wild in their own way. Anyone who enjoys nature will profit from every moment of their trip. You can even try your hand at fishing along the way.

But if you are in a hurry, if you seek an exciting life and fashionable resorts, then perhaps you will be bored with the tranquil water-routes. In the year 2000 this supreme luxury might become prohibitive in price. This is the luxury of peace that the canals of France offer you now.

1 · Summary of route details

Route No.		Rivers/Canals
1	**Agde** to **Royan** via Béziers, Carcassonne, Castelnaudary, Toulouse, Agen, Bordeaux	Canal du Midi, Canal latéral à la Garonne, River Garonne, River Gironde
1A	**Branch** from **Canal du Midi** to **La Nouvelle** via Narbonne	Canal de Jonction, River Aude, Canal de la Robine
2	**Beaucaire** to **Sète**	Canal du Rhône à Sète, Petit Rhône
3	**Berry-au-Bac** to **Maxilly-à-Saône** via Reims, Châlons-sur-Marne, Vitry-le-François, St Dizier, Chaumont, Langres	Canal de l'Aisne à Marne, Canal latéral à la Marne, Canal de la Marne à la Saône
4	**Berry-au-Bac** to **Troussey** via Rethel, Sedan, Commercy	Canal latéral à l'Aisne, Canal des Ardennes, Canal de l'Est
5	**Calais** to **Watten**	Canal du Calais, River Aa
5A	**Dunkirk** to **Watten**	Dunkerque – Escaut Waterway
6	**Chalon-sur-Saône** to **Lyon** via Mâcon, Villefranche-sur-Saône	River Saône

Route No.		Rivers/Canals
7	**Chauny** to **Berry-au-Bac**	Canal latéral à l'Oise, Canal de l'Oise à l'Aisne, Canal latéral à l'Aisne
8	**Chauny** to **Conflans St Honorine** via Compiègne, Pontoise	Canal latéral à l'Oise, River Oise
9	**Compiègne** to **Bourge-et-Comin** via Soissons	River Oise, River Aisne
10	**Laroche** to **Decize** via Auxerre, Clameçy	River Yonne, Canal du Nivernais
11	**Le Havre** to **Paris** via Roucn, Elbeuf, Vernon, Mantes	River Seine
12	**Lyon** to **Arles** via Vienne, Valence, Bollène, Avignon, Tarascon	River Rhône
12A	**Arles** to **Port St Louis**	River Rhône
13	**Messein** to **St Jean-de-Losne** via Epinal, Gray	Canal de l'Est, River Saône
14	**Paris** to **Condé** via Joinville, Meaux, Château-Thierry, Epernay, Ay	River Seine, River Marne
15	**Paris** to **St Mammes** via Melun	River Seine
16	**St Mammes** to **Chalon-sur-Saône** via Montargis, Briare, Nevers, Decize, Digoin, Montceau-les-Mines, Chagny	Canal du Loing, Canal de Briare, Canal latéral à la Loire, Canal du Centre
17	**St Mammes** to **Jean-de-Losne** via Sens, Joigny, Tonnerre, Montbard, Dijon	River Seine, River Yonne, Canal de Bourgogne

Route No.		Rivers/Canals
18	**St Nazaire** to **St Malo** via Nantes, Redon, Rennes, Dinan	River Loire, River Erdre, Canal de Nantes à Brest, River Vilaine, Canal d'Ille et Rance, River Rance
19	**St Valéry** to **St Simon** via Abbeville, Amiens, Péronne	Canal de la Somme
20	**Strasbourg** to **Chalon-sur-Saône** via Colmar, Mulhouse, Besançon, Dole	River Rhine, Grand Canal d'Alsace, Canal du Rhône au Rhin, River Saône
21	**Toul** to **Strasbourg** via Nancy	Canalized River Moselle, Canal de la Marne au Rhin
22	**Vitry-le-François** to **Messein** via Bar-le-Duc, Toul	Canal de la Marne au Rhin, Canalized Moselle, Canal de l'Est
23	**Watten** to **Chauny** via St Omer, Bethune, Lille, Cambrai, St Quentin	River Aa, Dunkerque-Escaut waterway, Canal de Saint-Quentin

From Belgium into France

BF/1	**Furnes** to **Dunkirk**	Canal de Nieuwpoort, Canal de Furnes
BF/2	**Menin** to **Armentières**	River Lys
BF/3	**Antoing** to **Douai**	River Escaut, River Scarpe
BF/4	**Antoing** to **Conde**	River Escaut

4 · Through the French Canals

Route No.		Rivers/Canals
BF5	**Blaton** to **Conde**	Canal de Pommeroeul à Antoing, Canal de Pommeroeul à Conde
BF/6	**Charleroi** to **Maubeuge**	River Sambre
BF/7	**Namur** to **Pont-a-Bar**	River Meuse
	From Germany and Luxembourg into France	
GLF/1	**Remerschen** to **Frouard**	River Moselle
	From Germany into France	
GF/2	**Kleinblittersdorf** to **Gondrexange**	River Saar, Canal des Houilleres de la Sarre
GF/3	**Lauterbourg** to **Strasbourg**	River Rhine

2 · Through routes to the Mediterranean

Through Route 1
Le Havre to the Mediterranean
via Canal de Bourgogne
Distance: **1348 km (838 M)**   Number of Locks: **243**   Tunnels: **1**
Minimum depth of water: **1.98 m**   Minimum height above waterline at normal water
level: **3.38 m**

Navigations	Towns and Villages	Route No
RIVER SEINE	Le Havre Paris	See Route 11
	Corbeil Melun St Mammes	See Route 15
RIVER YONNE	Montereau Pont-sur-Yonne Sens Joigny	See Route 17
CANAL DE BOURGOGNE	Laroche St Florentin Tonnerre Ravières Montbard Venarey Pouilley-en-Auxois	See Route 17
Tunnel	Dijon St Jean-de-Losne	
RIVER SAONE	Verdun Chalon-sur-Saône	See Route 20
	Lyon	See Route 6

Navigations	Towns and Villages	Route No
RIVER RHONE	**Vienne**	See
	Tournon	Route 12
	Valence	
	Avignon	
Craft proceeding *west* turn off before		
Arles into the *Petit Rhône*, see Route 2.		
	Arles	
Craft proceeding *east* continue down		See
the Rhône to	**Port St Louis**	Route 12A

This is the end of Rhône navigation.

Through Route 2
Le Havre to the Mediterranean
via The Bourbonnais

Distance: **842 miles**   Number of Locks: **180**   No tunnels
Minimum depth of water: **1.98 m**   Minimum height above waterline at normal water
level: **3.45 m**

Navigations	Towns and Villages	Route No
RIVER SEINE	**Le Havre**	See
	Paris	Route 11
	Corbeil	See
	Melun	Route 15
	St Mammes	
CANAL DU LOING	**Nemours**	See
CANAL DE BRIARE	**Buges**	Route 16
	Montargis	
	Briare	

Navigations	Towns and Villages	Route No.
CANAL LATERAL A LA LOIRE	Sancerre Nevers Decize	See Route 16
CANAL DU CENTRE	Digoin Montceau-les-Mines Chagny	See Route 16
RIVER SAONE	Châlon-sur-Saône	
	Lyon	See Route 6
RIVER RHONE	Vienne Tournon Valence Avignon	See Route 12
Craft proceeding *west* turn off before Arles into the *Petit Rhône*, see Route 2.	Arles	
Craft proceeding *east* continue down the Rhône to	Port St Louis	See Route 12A

This is the end of Rhône navigation.

Through Route 3
Le Havre to the Mediterranean
via Canal du Nivernais

Distance: 842 miles Number of Locks: **245** Tunnels: **1**
Minimum depth of water: **1.57 m** Minimum height above waterline at normal water level: **2.67 m**

Navigations	Towns and Villages	Route No
RIVER SEINE	Le Havre Paris	See Route 11

Navigations	Towns and Villages	Route No
	Corbeil	See
	Melun	Route 15
	St Mammes	
RIVER YONNE	Montereau	See
	Pont-sur-Yonne	Route 15
	Sens	
	Joigny	
	Laroche	
CANAL DU NIVERNAIS	Auxerre	See
	Clamecy	Route 10
	La Collancelle	
Tunnel	Mont-et-Marré	See
	Cercy-la-Tour	Route 10
	Decize	
CANAL LATERAL A LA LOIRE	Decize	See
CANAL DU CENTRE	Digoin	Route 16
	Montceau-les-Mines	
RIVER SAONE	Chalon-sur-Saône	
	Lyon	See Route 8
RIVER RHONE	Vienne	See
	Tournon	Route 12
	Valence	
	Avignon	
Craft proceeding *west* turn off before Arles into the *Petit Rhône*, see Route 2.	Arles	
Craft proceeding *east* continue down the Rhône to	Port St Louis	See Route 12A

This is the end of Rhône navigation.

Through Route 4
Le Havre to the Mediterranean
via The River Marne

Distance: **889 miles**   Number of Locks: **178**   tunnels: **4**
Minimum depth of water: **1.98 m**   Minimum height above waterline at normal water level: **3.45 m**

Navigations	Towns and Villages	Route No
RIVER SEINE	Le Havre	See
	Paris	Route 11
RIVER MARNE		
Tunnel		
	Joinville	See
	Lagny	Route 14
Tunnel		
	Meaux	
	Château Theirry	
	Epernay	
CANAL DE L'AISNE		
A LA MARNE	Condé	
CANAL LATERAL A LA MARNE	Chalons-sur-Marne	
	Vitry-le-François	
CANAL DE LA MARNE		
A LA SAONE	St Dizier	See
	Condes	Route 3
Tunnel		
	Chaumont	
	Langres	
	Batailes	
Tunnel		
RIVER SAONE	Heuilly	See
	Auxonne	Route 13
	St Jean-de-Losne	
	Verdun	See
	Chalon-sur-Saône	Route 20

Navigations	Towns and Villages	Route No
	Lyon	See Route 6
RIVER RHONE	Vienne Tournon Valence Avignon	See Route 12
Craft proceeding *west* turn off before Arles into the *Petit Rhône*, see Route 2.	Arles	
Craft proceeding *east* continue down the Rhône to	Port St Louis	See Route 12A

This is the end of Rhône navigation.

Through Route 5
Calais to the Mediterranean
Distance: **701 miles**   Number of Locks: **288**   Tunnels: **5**
Minimum depth of water: **1.98 m**   Minimum height above waterline at normal water level: **3.37 m**

Navigations	Towns and Villages	Route No.
CANAL DE CALAIS	Calais Pont-le-West Watten	See Route 5
DUNKERQUE-ESCAUT WATERWAY	Saint-Omer Aire-sur-la-Lys Bethune Bauvin Douai Corbehem Arleux	See Route 23

Navigations	Towns and Villages	Route No
RIVER ESCAUT CANAL DE SAINT-QUENTIN *Tunnel*	Cambrai Vendhuile Lesdins St Quentin St Simon	
CANAL DE L'OISE A L'AISNE *Tunnel*	Chauny Bichancourt Pargny-Filain Braye-en-Laonais Bourg-et-Comin	See Route 7
CANAL DE L'AISNE A LA MARNE CANAL LATERAL A LA MARNE *Tunnel*	Berry-au-Bac Reims Sept-Saulx Conde-sur-Marne Chalôns-sur-Marne Vitry-le-François	See Route 3
CANAL DE LA MARNE A LA SAONE *Tunnel* *Tunnel*	St-Dizier Joinville Bologne Chaumont Langres Balesmes-sur-Marne Heuilly-Cotton Maxilly-a-Saône	See Route 3
RIVER SAONE	Auxonne Chalon-sur-Saône	See Route 13 See Route 20

Navigations	Towns and Villages	Route No
	Lyon	See Route 6
RIVER RHONE	**Vienne** **Tournon** **Valence** **Avignon**	See Route 12
Craft proceeding *west* turn off before Arles into the *Petit Rhône*, see Route 2.		See Route 12A
	Arles	
Craft proceeding *east* continue down the Rhône to	**Port St Louis**	

This is the end of Rhône navigation.

3 · Stay in the inland waterways

On some occasions when the inland waterways of France are mentioned it is in connection with a passage to the Mediterranean, as though the waterways were only to be considered as a route to the sea. It is a pity that the Mediterranean casts such a spell, for that part of it within range of a cruise with limited time, has very little to offer the small boat owner compared with the peace and interest of the French canals.

Just as mountaineers have ambitions to get to the top of mountains so, it appears, do yachtsmen have ambitions to get to the Mediterranean; having achieved his ambition, the mountaineer simply returns. For the yachtsman the return is somewhat more involved, although a yacht with sufficient power can get back up the Rhône (of which more later). The knowledge and experience needed to get back via Biscay and St Malo is far greater than that needed for a cruise in the canals.

The Mediterranean has a great deal to offer the yachtsman with time to get far away from the crowded anchorages and harbours; or even for sailors who can afford to base their boats there. But for the more usual limited-time cruise, the time available would be far better spent exploring the inland waterways.

For instance, cruising in the Mediterranean you obviously have to seek a harbour when you want to stop. There is plenty of choice but not always with berths available. You will be lucky indeed if this berth happens to be clean, quiet, handy for getting ashore, near to shops; you will put up with these disadvantages rather than face the upheaval of going out again to seek another harbour that may be no better. In the canals you can stop practically where you like at any time.

The attractive harbours that you can reach within your time

allowance will be packed with other yachts. With the possible exception of Languedoc-Roussillon, the attractive and fashionable Mediterranean harbours have waiting lists for permanent moorings stretching into the years ahead. Visiting yachtsmen simply cannot be accommodated, except perhaps for a night stop after which a heavy charge is levied to ensure that visiting boats are kept on the move (and even this is not always possible in the peak holiday periods). Attractive canal stops are seldom crowded.

When cruising in the Mediterranean, you will have no choice but to go into many unattractive harbours. It is easy to forget, that there are undesirable features there, too. It will be a rare occasion indeed that you will need to stop in an unattractive place in the inland waterways.

Days spent cruising at sea are often a bore; in a sailing yacht the unpredictability of the wind is an irritation as well. Whether sailing or motor cruising it is easy to sympathize with the songwriter who wrote: 'we went to sea to see the world but all we saw was the sea'. I sympathize with the lady who said that she liked entering harbour and was quite interested in leaving harbour, but found the time in between a complete bore. There is no 'time in between' when you cruise in the inland waterways, for a whole panorama is unfolding at every moment – woods, towns, fields, little villages where you can step ashore to shop and explore.

At sea your progress is determined by weather; strong winds may suddenly appear, dying away to leave complete calm. Weather never interferes with your inland waterway progress (except at more or less predictable times of drought and flood). Waves knock you about at sea, particularly in the Mediterranean where they arrive violently and unexpectedly. In harbours the ships and fishing fleets churn up waves without consideration for the yachtsmen's slumbers. There are no waves in the waterways; the wash from passing craft is less than that in harbours, and on most of the waterways no traffic moves at night.

The distance down the Rhône from Lyon to the Mediterranean is around 320 km, a two to three day journey (although the powerful barges do it in half this time). As I explain in a later chapter, the business of cruising down the Rhône has been much simplified in recent years and, indeed, cruising up the Rhône has been made possible for most craft.

The expedition down the Rhône to 'see the sea' can use up time and effort and money which might be more profitably spent in the canals. So if you have limited time and budget consider, instead, a planned cruise through France. The Route Map (see pages viii–ix) shows the main navigable waterways of France arranged as 23 routes, connecting from one waterway junction to another. The towns and villages on or near each of these routes are also set out in detail in this section. Distances and the number of locks are shown.

For instance, if you plan to enter France at Le Havre, Route 11 will describe the route as far as Paris. If you wish to turn off before Paris, you can do so at Conflans-St Honorine (Route 8), up, say to Compiègne, branching right on Route 9 to Bourg-et-Comin, continuing on Route 7 to Berry-au-Bac, turning right on Route 3 as far as Conde-sur-Marne where you may take Route 14 to Paris; then back on Route 11 to return to Le Havre and you will have covered 1071 km, passed through 69 locks, and sampled a little champagne on the way, perhaps.

Route No		Km	Locks
11	Le Havre to Conflans River Seine	290	6
	Turn left		
8	Conflans to Compiègne River Oise	93	7
	Turn right		
9	Compiègne to Bourg-et-Comin River Aisne	64	7
	Continue		
7	Bourg-et-Comin to Berry-au-Bac Canal latéral à l'Aisne	21	1

Route No		Km	Locks
3	*Turn right* Berry-au-Bac to Condé-sur-Marne Canal de l'Aisne à Marne	58	26
14	*Turn right* Condé to Paris River Marne	183	15
11	Paris to Le Havre River Seine	362	7
		1071	69

How long does it take?

The length of time this would take would obviously depend upon the number of hours you wished to spend in cruising every day, but my wife and I would reckon to make it a reasonable three to four weeks' cruise.

Many permutations and combinations of other routes can be planned along these lines; but the main point to be borne in mind is that anyone with even three or four weeks to spare can enjoy a cruise in the French canals. Cruises can be tailor-made to fit in with the time available.

In order to plan what distance you can cruise in the time you have available, you would not be far out if you reckoned upon averaging 4 knots between locks and thirty minutes to pass through each lock. (This is simply a rough average for planning purposes only. At some of the bigger locks a wait of several hours is not uncommon.) Some routes have many more locks than others and how many you can manage in a day depends upon the number of your crew and their agility.

It is usual to average around fifteen to twenty locks a day once you get used to the physical exertion involved. Moving a boat through locks is not a particularly strenuous occupation but after your first few days you realize what sort of physical condition you are in. It is wise to take it easy at first.

Speed limits

Speed limits are as follows:

Canals		$3\frac{1}{4}$	knots
Seine	20 tonnes and over	$13\frac{1}{2}$	knots
	When passing	8	knots
	10 tonnes and over	8	knots upstream
		$9\frac{3}{4}$	knots downstream
	In Paris	$6\frac{1}{2}$	knots
Rhône		$13\frac{1}{2}$	knots
	When passing	8	knots
Marne		$6\frac{1}{2}$	knots
General limit		6	knots

The canal speed limit of just over 3 knots does not seem to be very closely observed by commercial traffic. In some of the narrower canals a speed of 5 knots can set up a considerable wash, and where damage to the banks is likely to result you should slow down. Wherever the wash of your craft is likely to inconvenience others you should also slow down, in fact you should use your judgement and show consideration at all times. It will be seen that speed limits in the rivers are higher than in the canals but, whenever you are in doubt, you can use the barges as your guide.

Maps and guide books

In planning your cruise it will pay to consult as many maps and guide books as possible so that you go through, and near, most places of interest. The Michelin sectional maps are so useful for this purpose that the appropriate sectional map numbers have been placed against each place name shown in the Route Details Section. If you write to the local *Syndicats d'Initiative* of the towns along your planned route they will be pleased to send you information regarding items of interest in their area and of events taking place at the time of your proposed visit. Minutes spent in advance planning will repay with hours of interest and pleasure on the cruise. Somehow this planning seems to be more worthwhile with a cruise than with a motor tour, maybe because you cruise along the waterways in such a leisurely fashion that stopping is no inconvenience, and you get used to stopping for locks anyhow.

Cruising the French canals is the most delightful experience, catering for every taste; an active holiday for the active and a leisurely one for the leisurely, all rolled into one.

To get the most out of your exploring you need a bicycle for each person on board; a place on deck can usually be found for them. The Michelin maps show all the byways, and coasting along the country lanes to shop at out of the way villages is a delight. There will be no shortage of volunteers to pedal along some grassy towpath in the clear morning air to fetch the bread and milk. Shopping bags are no weight on the handlebars. When water and fuel have to be carried any distance the bike will be worth its weight in Puligny-Montrachet. And if you wish to make quicker progress through some relatively uninteresting section, a crew member can easily cycle ahead along the towpath to prepare the locks for your coming.

Having planned your route you will obviously want to stick to it when you arrive in France or your planning will be very largely wasted.

The details given against the place names in the Route Details Section are not by any means comprehensive, but it is hoped that the brief data given will arouse your interest sufficiently for you to want to seek further information. At each of the places named, whether described or not, it is understood that at least a shop will be nearby, and usually there will be much more.

Boat handling skills

No special skill is needed to handle a boat on the French canals. Any active couple with the ability to navigate a car will find no difficulty in handling a motor cruiser. If you doubt this, consider the tens of throusands who drive a motor cruiser for the first time on the Norfolk Broads or on the Thames. There is a pointer in one French canal cruise holiday brochure that states 'previous cruising experience (though not essential) is an asset'.

I have met perhaps a dozen brave or foolhardy folk who have crossed the Channel in their first sailing boat, having had no experience whatever before setting out. However, I do not recommend that anyone without experience, setting out on a cruise of the French canals, should cross the Channel unaccompanied from England. But I would repeat again and again that the biggest factor in the whole business of going off on a worthwhile cruise is the making of the decision to do it.

Perhaps the hesitant by nature always stand too much in awe of experience. Put out of your mind that great intelligence or ability is needed to navigate or to handle a boat. Professional skippers are no Einsteins, and as for the amateurs, an hour in a marina watching the mooring antics would convince you that many existing yachtsmen deserve to be carrying L-plates.

Make up your mind that you can master boat handling and you will; if you have an experienced friend to help you, so much the better. The important thing to acquire in your own home cruising area is the ability to handle your boat precisely. Common sense conquers most problems once you can handle your boat with certainty.

What sort of person goes cruising on the inland waterways of France? One of the many pleasant features of cruising life is that you make friends immediately when you stop by another boat; but if it was possible to analyse all the gossiping that we have

Cycle along the grassy towpath for bread and milk in the morning.

done in this way over the years, I do not think that any particular age group or type of person would emerge.

If the cruising life attracts all ages and types, there is one thing, at least, that most have in common, and that is the ability to get on with one another. If this quality is not very apparent at the beginning of a cruise it will certainly blossom during it. A boat is a wonderful place for developing a deeper understanding of one another; in the confinement of a cabin you simply have to get on together, and most people do.

4 · Suitable and unsuitable boats

Power or sail?

What boat should you choose? Sail or power? New or second-hand? If you are a beginner you will obviously have less to learn if you buy a motor cruiser rather than a sailing yacht; but this consideration cannot be of the greatest importance because beginners are sailing away in sailing yachts every day of the week.

Quite apart from the relative merits of sailing versus motor cruising, a motor cruiser will have roomier accommodation for a given overall length than a sailing boat. The sailing boat hull needs to be a 'sailing shape' whereas the motor cruising hull does not need such fine underwater lines. The comparatively restricted accommodation of a sailing yacht is further reduced by the stowage room needed for sails and gear. The cockpit space needed for managing the business of sailing can be used for accommodation in a motor cruiser.

You would only buy a sailing boat if you were keen to enjoy sailing at times when you were not inland cruising. At these times the handling of a sailing boat involves your family, for one member usually attends to sail changing while another minds the helm. In a motor cruiser, only the one person at the wheel is involved.

These are all general considerations to be borne in mind and do not refer specifically to selecting the most suitable craft in which to explore the French canals; for this purpose alone there is no doubt that a motor cruiser would be the obvious choice.

Unstepping masts

If, however, you feel that you would like to sail sometimes and explore the inland waterways on other occasions, then there is no difficulty in unstepping the mast of a suitable sailing yacht when you want to use it for canal cruising. Big sailing yachts with tall masts would obviously not be suitable for the inland waterways because of their deep draft. In addition to this, no sailing yacht whose mast height greatly exceeds the LOA of the boat should be selected as a canal cruiser; apart from being a nuisance when manoeuvring, the overhang can easily cause damage, not only to the overhanging section, but to the whole mast and to everything to which it is attached.

Most entry ports into France have yacht clubs where masts cannot only be unstepped, but stored. In Le Havre, for instance, this can be arranged at the Petit Port by the *Capitaine du Port* on the quay from whom you book a time for going under the crane.

In ports where a crane is not available it is quite often possible to go alongside a British merchant ship to have the lift made by the ship's derrick. If neither crane nor derrick is available there will always be some convenient height nearby from which to exert the necessary leverage and control. A bridge over the waterway is ideal. Spare blocks and suitable rope should be carried for rigging up a pulley arrangement (tackle) to the bridge; the right-size trestles for stowing the mast on deck should be made up before leaving home.

Multihulls

Before considering specific craft it should be mentioned that catamarans are not suitable for cruising the French canals by reason of their beam; averaging nearly half of the LOA, this beam would prevent entry into the small space often left for pleasure craft in the busier commercial locks. On the narrower waterways, passing other craft would present problems. Many catamarans have made passages through the French canals, but I would not recommend them as a suitable choice.

Trimarans, with a beam often equal to almost two-thirds of their LOA, would not even get into the majority of the locks.

Prop power

The ideal craft is a twin-screw motor cruiser with inside and outside steering positions and controls, but only if it is a craft with propellers protected, either by the sort of metal guards that you see on barges or by the actual position of the propellers in the shape of the hull. If a propeller is so sited that it is the first thing to touch the sloping side of a lock, the boat is going to need plenty of spare propellers.

The same objections, indeed more so, apply to outdrives, inboard/outboards, transom, stern drives, or whatever other name is given to outside drive units, to my mind unsuitable for the French canals. I have seen them caught on the sills of descending locks and am convinced that the less you have 'outside' of your boat the less likely you are to run into trouble. Even if remote controls could bring outside drive units completely inboard, instead of raising them, the point is that there is rarely any advance warning of the time when this might be necessary.

Protection is, therefore, essential for any yacht with exposed propellers. If you have a choice between single or twin, single is perfectly adequate for the French canals, and obviously more economical. A twin screw is more manoeuvrable, although a good skipper will manage a single screw better than a poorer one with a twin. In recent years bow thrusters have appeared on quite small craft and this is certainly a splendid aid to manoeuvring, particularly in confined harbours and waterways. It is also less expensive to fit a single engine and bow thruster rather than twin engines.

Professional advice

Many people write to ask me what is the most suitable craft for them and I am happy to oblige. I need to know how many there will be in the crew, how much money it is proposed to spend, and the extent of sailing or cruising experience.

It is hardly necessary for me to stress, I hope, that you should never buy a second-hand boat without a professional survey.

The RYA has long been active in protecting the rights of yachtsmen and if you are not a member may I suggest that you join and thus help the cause. The address is Royal Yachting Association, Romsey Rd, Eastleigh, Hants SO5 4YA and they are always most helpful and willing to advise you on the current situation regarding documentation needed for craft entering France (and, of course, on many other matters). Indeed, as you

probably know, the RYA has been the provider of acceptable
'papers' for unregistered craft entering France for many years.
If, in your case, these 'papers' take the form of the Small Ships
Registry, these are currently being supervised by the DVLA,
Swansea, SA99 1BX. Such registry bears an expiry date,
although no renewal notices are issued.

Comfort and safety

In considering a suitable boat for the waterways you will be
thinking in terms of living onboard for several weeks at a time
and you will want as much room as you can afford, certainly
headroom. An aft cabin is a good idea for families with children
or for two families. It also makes for easier living to have the
separate bedroom that an aft cabin makes possible. Two toilets
make for harmony, two toilets *and* showers make for luxury
indeed, but naturally you have to watch the water supply,
pumps, heaters, drain away.

The ideal accommodation layout that has developed in
suitable motor cruisers provides a bedroom or cabin at either
end of the boat, each with its own toilet and shower; a central
galley with dinette opposite which makes up into a double berth
and a secondary steering position on the aft deck.

You should bear in mind the question of freeboard when you
are going about the delightful business of choosing your dream
yacht for the French waterways. The seller of any 'high-out-of-
the-water' dream yacht will have thoughtfully provided a
stepped platform alongside for your ease of access and descent
when you come to view; but when emergencies arise later and
you need to quickly leap off or on there will be no one alongside
with a stepped platform. You will need to be stepping off and on
at high speed on occasions and you should choose a boat that
allows all of your crew to do this easily.

Draft above and below the water

Shallow draft or bilge keel craft are an advantage in the
waterways because they enable you to go alongside attractive
river banks and villages denied to a deeper draft. For the ideal
French waterway yacht I think that a 1.2 m (4 ft) draft is about
right despite the average waterway depth of two metres. I have

The British built steel Hylander, a suitable craft for the waterways.

taken yachts drawing 1.6 m (5 ft 6 ins) plus through the waterways without trouble but with such a draft one's stopping places are limited. Retractable keels are not often seen but they are eminently suitable.

The most critical dimension is air draft, or height above the water. The modern design tendency of British motor cruiser builders is to provide a flying bridge which debars the majority of popular cruisers from the French inland waterways. When salesmen tell you that their boat will go through the French canals, they are referring to the main routes to the Mediterranean but, even here, the Burgundy Canal minimum bridge height is 3.38 m (11 ft 1 in), the Bourbonnais is 3.45 m (11 ft 3 in), the Canal du Nivernais 2.67 m (under 10 ft), the Marne 3.45 m (11 ft 3 in), and from Calais 3.37 m (11 ft 1 in). Every waterway height above the waterline is shown in the following Route Details Section, and you should study them before falling in love with a boat that is too high out of the

The moment of truth – when you wish you'd paid more attention to air draft. (The Canal du Nivernais.)

water. It does mean that the large majority of cruisers on sale in the UK are unsuitable for the European inland waterways.

Cruising in retirement

Many more people approaching retirement are now seeking to spend their early retired years in cruising the European waterways and wintering in the Mediterranean. 'For a year or so, maybe', they protest tentatively, but years later I receive cards from happy, bronzed nautical tramps who could never consider giving up the marine gipsy life and whose only regret is that they did not embark upon it years earlier.

An odd observation, but one that my wife and I have made frequently, is that personal relationships improve when confined to the waterway life. You would imagine the reverse to be the case, indeed we have all heard women protesting that 'they do not know what they will do when they are shut up with him all day long on his retirement' – and they are usually referring to life in a house! The intimacy of the boating life must act like an emotional pressure cooker bringing out only the best; we have seen the most unlikely couples wandering ashore hand in hand . . .

When you plan on boating in retirement you must plan for comfort first of all. You can forget all about sailing on your ear. Make sure you have a superb kitchen and dining area, a comfortable bedroom, toilet and shower and then – and only then – can you start deciding how much sailing performance and paraphernalia you can wrap around that.

Even for those who openly object to sailing, who have simply never gone along with boating ideas at all, there is still the avenue of persuasion represented by the inland waterways of Europe. Obviously you would not go across Seine Bay by way of introduction; but to have the boat alongside some charming French village where you have arranged for dinner ashore perhaps, and then next day to commence gliding through the beauty of France, bounce-free and passing by a never ending panorama of interest . . . you can more easily than you think have anyone hooked on the boating life. By the time you get to the Mediterranean the boat will have become a way of life and the odd bounce will be accepted.

By the time you get to the Mediterranean you will also be very much fitter and perhaps this is the time to mention that if you have been accustomed to a sedentary life you should retire to the boating life by easy stages. If you make yourself competent at handling your craft, the passage through the many locks should present no physical stresses but after the first few days of rope throwing and hauling and maybe some lock ladder climbing you can expect to be exhausted. Then after a day of rest and recovery and a bottle or so of Côtes du Rhône you recover; you will not fully enjoy the French canals if you try to do too much too soon.

Your choice of boat is all important from the point of view of conservation of energy, and the less agile you are the more you must consider this aspect when choosing your boat. When I am asked to find a suitable craft, one of the first considerations I take into account is the physical capability of the buyer and the crew in relation to the boat to be chosen. I make no apology for emphasizing that if you choose a boat that is 'too much for you' your European waterway adventures will be more stress and strain than pleasure; if you choose a boat that is totally within your physical control and capability your European waterway cruises will fulfil your pleasantest dreams.

5 · The taming of the Rhône

I do not believe that such a vast achievement as the taming of the Rhône should be taken for granted, however, and I feel that every user of this waterway should be aware of the vision, enterprise, courage and effort of the Frenchmen who created it. I am indebted to the Compagnie Nationale du Rhône *who have kindly supplied me with the information contained in this chapter.*

In previous editions I referred to the Rhône as a 'slippery slope'; the inference being that once one left Lyon and passed through the Pierre-Bénite Lock to embark on the downstream passage of the Rhône, for most craft it was a one-way journey, as most craft would not possess the power to get up again. Going down has never been a problem; unless you count as problems raging torrents, midstream rocks, wildly varying depths of water, shifting sandbanks and banks of mud and gravel.

Although smallest of the three principal river basins of France, the Rhône in former days presented many difficulties to navigation. Apart from the speed and irregularity of the Rhône current, shipping was further hazarded by the formation of gravel banks, aided by the Alpine 'feeders' Isère and Durance bringing down large amounts of mud, gravel and flood water from melted snow; the Cévennes streams, Ardèche and Gard, on the right bank also caused sudden rises and falls.

The giant power of the river has always been utilized to sweep man and cargoes down from Lyon to the sea. This power has its origins in the greenish ice of the Rhône Glacier, barely fifty miles from the origin of the north-flowing Rhine. By the Belvedere Inn on the Funka Pass in the Swiss Alps a stream comes rushing out that is the beginning of the mighty Rhône. Spring sunshine melts the Alpine snows and through meadows dotted with blue gentian, yellow mountain saxifrage and dark red dwarf primula, the river gathers strength and is joined by other streams from the mountains on both sides.

At the town of Brig, 45 km (28 M) from its source, the Rhône has already dropped 1220 m (4000 ft). By the time it reaches Lake Geneva it has travelled 170 km (105 M), all too swift and too steep for navigation. At the other end of the lake, 72 km (45 M) across, locks take over control. When 19 km (12 M) from Geneva, the Rhône becomes French and is immediately put to work; a few miles inside the French border is the huge Genissiat Dam.

Coming up has always been the ordeal and upstream traffic has been negligible. Until the advent of steam it took thirty or forty horses to tow one barge up to Lyon. The difficulties were so considerable that many cargoes were despatched downstream on collapsible rafts that were dismantled at the Mediterranean end. Then steam power took over from the horse and from the collapsible raft. Rhône navigation became of great importance during the first half of the 19th century. Then the Marseille-Lyon railway opened and Rhône navigation suffered a virtual collapse.

At the end of the century the industrial potential of hydro-electricity was realized; the energy producing possibilities of the Rhône – coupled with the transformation of the agriculture of the valley by the development of an irrigation system – developed the river into an international waterway. These considerations resulted in the 'Rhône formula' by which the river would be developed by means of the profits received from hydro-electricity.

A law was passed in 1921 granting development powers to various interests. Discussions and negotiations ensued. In 1933 the *Compagnie Nationale du Rhône* was created with the stature of a limited company, a 'Company of General Interest'. In 1934 the CNR received the general concession for the development of the Rhône; it was a company with the characteristics of a limited company, with a capital of 24 million francs divided into 2,400,000 shares! A company in which the following local interests participated:

- The Department of the Seine, a large consumer of energy.
- The Department, Communes, Chambers of Commerce and Chambers of Agriculture of the Rhône Valley.

- The Paris-Lyon-Mediterranée Railway Company (foreseeing the electrification of the Paris–Marseille line).
- Companies involved in transport and electricity.

In 1937 the railways were nationalized and the PLM became the SNCF. In 1946 electricity was nationalized and *Electricité de France* became the interested party in that sphere.

CNR conforms in certain aspects to a nationalized company. The government guarantees borrowing since the profits made from the sale of the Rhône energy must be used to benefit navigation and agriculture. The CNR may not charge tolls for navigating the Rhône nor for agricultural use of the water.

CNR's general programme included the construction of 21 combined developments (grouping primarily barrages, dammed reservoirs, diversion canals, navigation locks, works assuring drainage) which principally feed nineteen major hydro-electric stations, seven of which are situated on the Upper Rhône above Lyon, the other twelve being on the Lower Rhône.

The impressive figures of electric energy production envisaged are outside the scope of these comments. From the navigation point of view the first priority was to be given to the construction of a waterway with a complete canal system stretching 310 km (192 M) in length from Lyon to the Mediterranean (Port St Louis du Rhône).

The creation of surrounding port zones and industrial zones was envisaged, increased possibilities for irrigation and the consequent improvement of agriculture, protection against flooding, stabilization of the water table and the creation of nautical facilities.

From the outset the CNR's interest in Rhône navigation was demonstrated with the construction of Port Edouard Herriot, in a suburb south of Lyon, directly below the junction of the Rhône and Saône rivers. Begun in 1934, the port was put into full operation in 1973 (having been considerably enlarged in 1966).

Construction of the Genissiat (1937–1948) and Seyssel (1951) barrages do not concern us here since they are situated in the gorges of the Upper Rhône and were created purely for hydro-electric potential.

Development of the central portion of the Lower Rhône, between Isère and Ardèche, took place between 1947 and 1968. In 1947 construction began at Donzère-Mondragon, after which developments at Montélimar, Baix-Le-Logis Neuf, Beauchastel and Bourg-les-Valence proceeded. To illustrate the scale of this gigantic project it may be of interest to mention the detail involved in one construction. Five years of effort (1947–1952) at Donzère-Mondragon created the following major projects: the reservoir-barrage, raising the water level by 5 m (16 ft) at low water and producing a dammed reservoir of approximately 10 km (6 M). The diversion canal, short circuiting 31 km (18 M) of the river, including a 17 km (10 M) lead-in canal and an 11 km (7 M) escape canal. The intake of water feeding the lead-in canal includes two branches; a navigable branch, wide and not very deep, allowing for the passage of one-third of the flow; the other branch handling the other two-thirds. The lock allows for a difference in level of 26 m (85 ft)! The ability to rapidly fill and empty the lock chambers of a capacity of almost 60 000 m³ without noticeable effect on the water level was solved in ingenious fashion.

The building of Donzère-Mondragon took a work force of 6800 which, with their families, meant that over 10 000 people had to be accommodated in new sites built nearby.

The **Montélimar** development (1953–1957) included an intake of Rhône water at right angles to Rochemaure and a diversion canal close to 14 km (8 M) in length on the left bank of the Rhône. The lock allows for a difference in level of 19 m (62 ft). The works of the central third of the Rhône were completed with the opening of **Baix-le-Logis Neuf** in 1960, **Beauchastel** in 1963 (the only development whose diversion is on the right bank of the Rhône) and **Bourg-les-Valence** in 1968; each with an average drop of 11–12 m (36–39 ft).

At Baix-le-Logis Neuf, the junction of the Drôme was made to take place in the reservoir. At Bourg-les-Valence the Isère was absorbed in the canal; the central portion of the lead-in canal being, in fact, the lowest riverbed of the Isère.

Whilst the central part was being developed, an even more ambitious project was taking place on the Rhône immediately downstream with its junction with the Saône. This development

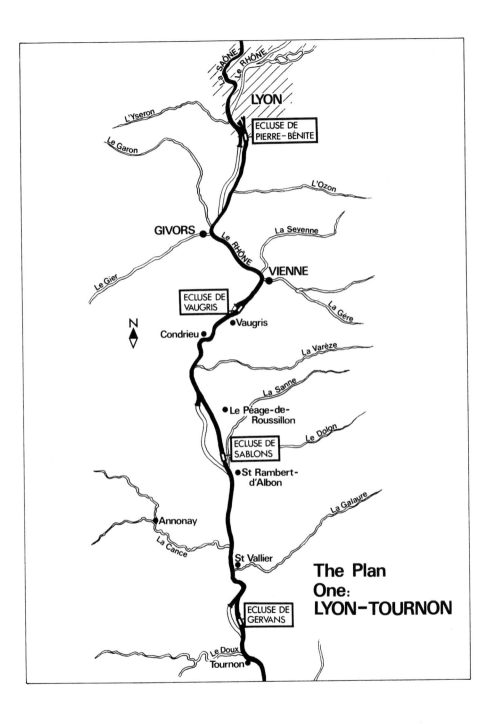

The Plan
One:
LYON–TOURNON

at **Pierre-Bénite** (1962–1966), established a continuous canal reach of 21 km (13 M) on the Rhône and the Saône up to the lock at Couzon and did away with two old locks on the Saône at La Mulatière and Ile-Barbe. In this way Pierre-Bénite became the unifying link for the Port of Lyon and the rivers Rhône and Saône. (The works at Pierre-Bénite also provided excavated material on which was built the huge Rhône-Alps Refinery at Feyzin and transformed a deserted and marshy region, ravaged by Rhône floods, into an industrial zone.)

Completion of the Rhône developments below Lyon were considered with an industrial application for creating a steel industry at Fos and for increasing the transport capacity of the Rhône from 15 million tonnes per year to over 50 million tonnes per year with the doubling of locks.

Vallabrègues (1966–1970) extended the drop from Avignon to Tarascon-Beaucaire in a flat plain of negligible decline. This development canalized the river for 34 km (21 M). Although the earthworks moved and materials used at Vallabrègues were comparable to those at Donzère-Mondragon, the workforce never exceeded 1800 as opposed to the 6800 employed at Donzère-Mondragon; increased productivity resulted in 33 months being spent at Vallabrègues compared to 50 months at Donzère-Mondragon. Hence within the space of 15 years the manpower needed for construction could be reduced in the ratio of 6:1.

Saint Vallier (1969–1973) is characterized by its long reservoirs between Saint-Rambert d'Albon and Serves and short diversion. The drop varies between 10 m (33 ft) and 11.5 m (38 ft). This operation lengthened the continuous canalization of the Rhône to 134 km (83 M) from the 115 km (71 M) at Mondragon.

At Le Palier d'Arles (1971–1973) it was a question of developing the Rhône riverbed by dredging, between the restoration of water at Vallabrègues and the Petit Rhône up to the region at **St Gilles**. (From then it was no longer possible to lock through from the Rhône into the Canal du Rhône à Sète at Beaucaire.) Joining of the Rhône canal at Sète by means of the new lock saw the beginning of the international use of this waterway.

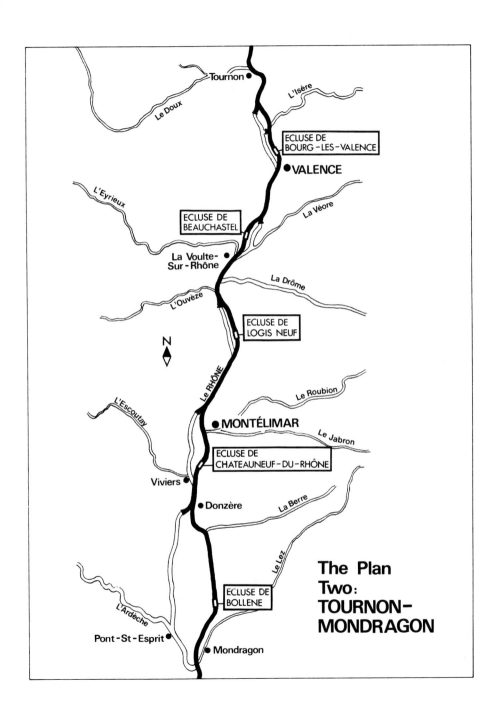

Tournon

L'Isère

Le Doux

ECLUSE DE
BOURG – LES – VALENCE

● VALENCE

L'Eyrieux

La Véore

ECLUSE DE
BEAUCHASTEL

La Voulte-
Sur - Rhône

La Drôme

L'Ouvèze

ECLUSE DE
LOGIS NEUF

N

Le RHÔNE

Le Roubion

L'Escoutay

● MONTÉLIMAR

Le Jabron

ECLUSE DE
CHATEAUNEUF – DU – RHÔNE

Viviers

● Donzère

La Berre

Le Lez

The Plan
Two:
TOURNON-
MONDRAGON

ECLUSE DE
BOLLENE

L'Ardèche

Pont - St - Esprit

● Mondragon

The **Avignon** (1971–1973) development included a dammed reservoir over 10 km (6 M) in length.

The opening of **Caderousse** removed the last remaining obstacle to navigation on the downstream third of the Rhône. The joining achieved by this lock between the developed sections of the downstream third and central third created an uninterrupted distance of 249 km (154 M) between the Mediterranean and St Rambert d'Albon.

Le Peage-de-Rousilion (1973–1974) includes a dammed reservoir extending for 25 km (15 M) and a diversion canal 11 km (7 M) in length.

Vaugris (at K 33) involved the section of the river between Pierre-Bénite and Condrieu; this was the last link in the chain between the Mediterranean and Lyon, a total distance of 310 km (192 M). Although it was only a short section that remained uncompleted, and the temporary channel round was quite straightforward, it seemed to remain uncompleted for a long time, arousing anxieties in the minds of Rhône-cruising yachtsmen out of proportion to the 20 km (12 M) involved. But now it is done.

And now you can get back up the Rhône . . . *if* you can make 7 knots that is. At times your speed over the ground will appear to be negligible but for almost the whole distance the flow will be smooth and controlled and calm looking. The surging, soaring passage of yesterday is forgotten.

But the current still runs strongly and before you undertake a passage of the Rhône, either up or down, you should ensure that the engine of your craft is in good order; a broken fan belt, dirty fuel or blocked filter in the cooling system can be unfortunate at any time but would easily spell disaster on the Rhône.

However confident you are in the efficiency of your engine(s) you must have anchor and chain ready; if you had to use it it might not hold but at least it would swing you round and check you. Steering as though going ahead, at least you would have a chance of avoiding the piers of bridges, etc. It is a good idea to make the passage of the Rhône in company with another yacht so that in the event of engine failure one can help by 'supplying brakes' to the other.

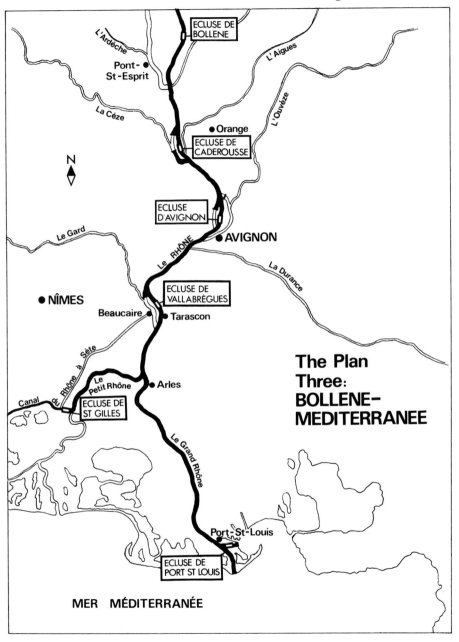

The Plan
Three:
**BOLLENE-
MEDITERRANEE**

It is not necessary now to employ a pilot. But take care, particularly in the short, uncanalized section.

You must also be sure that you have adequate fuel, taking spare cans onboard if necessary. The withdrawal of FOD (*fuel oil doméstique*) for use in pleasure craft is mentioned elsewhere, but the difficulties of obtaining petrol are noticeable between Chalon-sur-Saône and Port St Louis.

On the Bollène-Mediterranean section of the Rhône map (as on other maps), you will see that the river is shown as flowing straight down to the Mediterranean as indeed it does or, at least, it finally spreads its way there. But, in fact, the final section of the Rhône is not a waterway to anywhere for traffic intending to 'turn right' has already done so at the Petit Rhône and traffic intending to 'turn left' has already done so at Port St Louis. Even in this area the river is already between half a mile and a mile wide in places; down the final 6 km (4 M), below Port St Louis, the mighty Rhône finally dissipates itself fanwise in separate and changing and unchartered streams; all we found was a nowhere of desolation, even by Camargue standards, shifting sands and silt pushing ever seawards.

6 · Equipment

On cruising into the beautiful waterways of France you can forget all about plotting courses, and fixes, and sail changing, bouncing around and hanging on. You can forget all about the need to work out your direction – it is there, ahead, the water-road referred to by Georges Normand in his introduction.

The equipment needed will be for: protecting your yacht against the odd encounter with other craft and with lock walls, providing adequate securing and getting ashore facilities, fuel and water transport, and safety onboard.

Fenders and planks

Adequate fenders are necessary, a minimum of four, large, sausage shape, but preferably more because they can come under considerable strain when being squeezed along the sides of steel barges. And they can be easily broken off on entering those locks where it is necessary to put a crew member ashore with a warp; for the lock ladder is usually just inside beyond the lock gate and in manoeuvring to put your crew on the ladder you must obviously be close in, so close that fenders get pressed into the gate recess and held there while the yacht moves on. It does not often happen, but there are times when concentration wavers, for instance when you are nearing the end of the thirty-seven locks (which are almost joined together) approaching the summit of the Bourgogne.

Fender sox are a useful addition to protect your boat in grimy locks. A plank or two comes in very useful for hanging outside the fenders when alongside pontoons or piles that otherwise work their way inside the protective fenders and make contact with the hull. The plank is sure to come in handy doubling up as a gangplank when, for some reason, there is too big a gap between the boat and the shore. A hole in each end of the plank will make for easy attachment.

Sometimes, when it is desirable to come alongside an unscalable quay wall, a ladder onboard then makes all the difference between getting ashore and not.

Boathooks, stakes and warps

Take the largest boathook you can conveniently stow on deck. If you are a congenital boathook loser, take two. If you have only one, obtain a long pole on the canal bank as soon as you can. Lock-keepers in the country sections invariably have a fine selection. You will need the pole for fending off, not only from the walls of locks with sloping sides, but from canal banks when you secure in just sufficient depth of water. You see barges moored in this way with poles almost big enough to do duty carrying telephone wires.

You will need two stakes, preferably of metal; these you will find useful, necessary even, to hammer into the bank alongside when there is no other attachment for your warps. Also, of course, you will need a mallet or large hammer for banging the stakes into the ground.

Warps have a hard working life on the waterways and I consider that four 27 m (15 fathom) 38 mm (1½ in) to 50 mm (2 in) warps are the minimum that should be carried on an average cruiser of around 8 tonnes. Every lock puts a strain on them that they do not experience in harbour. The water surges to or from the lock and I watch the warps straining, sometimes chafing over the edge of a lock wall, finding sharp cracks and crevices. Warps are your waterway friends and you should look after them most attentively.

Dinghies

I have read accounts of people who have towed dinghies through the inland waterways, and I cannot imagine anything so calculated to cause anxiety. Sometimes when entering locks, there is only just enough room for you to squeeze your boat in; in such circumstances, a dinghy towed astern would certainly be in danger of being crushed between the lock gates. Passing on narrow waterways would be made much more difficult if allowance had to be made for a dinghy weaving about astern on the wash from the barge and the return wash from the bank. You never, never see a barge or other commercial craft towing a dinghy on the inland waterways for this reason. Yet one must have a dinghy so it must be capable of being stowed inboard out of the way. I have come to the conclusion over the years that an inflatable is the answer. At sea we keep our inflatable on the foredeck fully inflated; in the event of having to 'take to the boats' we know that there is sufficient buoyancy to support us. We feel particularly strongly about this, having had a wooden dinghy sink under us; and if my wife and I had not been able to swim our cruising days would have ended. The advantage of an inflatable is that when we enter the inland waterways we are able to stow it in its bag and put it out of the way.

Flags and sirens

As far as flags are concerned, a French courtesy flag will be needed, of course, and a Q flag. You might be glad of international code flag G if you find yourself in need of a pilot; in the waterways you would step ashore and find one.

You will need a hooter or siren to warn of your approach. In the peace of the country locks you could almost shout to announce your arrival, but in the commercial sections and harbours, with noise all around, you need something fairly drastic. We have a compressed air siren with a renewable container. Although no bigger than a cocoa tin, it lets off such a blast that I sometimes feel self-conscious about using it. But it works.

Torches and searchlights

Two or three good torches are necessary, for you will often be returning to your boat at night, perhaps on unlighted canal banks. Replacement batteries and torches are easy enough to buy anywhere in France.

A good searchlight with a wide beam will be essential for the tunnels. In some tunnels you can be towed if you have no searchlight, or if the light you have is considered unsatisfactory. Towing times and charges are available at the lock nearest the entrance.

Containers and hoses

The only other necessary items that might be classed as deck equipment are portable containers for fuel, water, and paraffin, as many as you can stow. There are so many different shapes and sizes of container that it is well worth going to the trouble of finding ones that fit your available stowage space; you will also need filling funnels for each. A boat hose is also worth investing in for use with lock-side water taps. The type that packs flat on a reel is best. Obtain a variety of fittings, the best type being push-on rubber ones, secured with a jubilee clip or butterfly screw. Also, your filler caps should be attached inboard by a wire or line.

Unstepping masts

Sailing yachts will need stowage planned in advance on deck for the mast when it is unstepped. Trestles at each end of the boat are simplest, with the centre of the mast resting on the top of the coachroof, in the tabernacle if there is a convenient one. Pieces of foam rubber are useful for protecting the masts at points of contact and at each end if there is an overhang. I am often asked if the overhang of masts presents a problem in going through the waterways. I have taken a boat through with an overhang of 2.5 m at each end and I would say that this is about the limit one should contemplate. The difficulty arises in the smaller locks when you are below the level of the lock wall, and the rush of water causes the boat to swing strongly. Stationing oneself right forward with a boathook at the ready is the answer but it can be a bit of a strain at times.

I have seen boats with timber lashed athwart the bows when the overhang of the mast is considerable. This prevents damage to the mast by swinging in locks but such an arrangement is viewed with apprehension by other craft alongside.

Sailing yachts should take a supply of strong, stringed labels to mark each item of standing and running rigging, blocks and shackles before the mast is unstepped; as soon as it is laid on the deck the shambles of rigging will resemble a fallen tree. A few spare mast bolts are worth taking in case a replacement is needed.

Of the two sailing cruisers shown sharing a lock on the Canal d'Ille et Rance in Brittany, that on the right has removed its mast altogether, while the other boat has lowered its mast on to specially constructed wooden crutches. *Photo Hugh McKnight*

Masts can be left at the yacht compound in the Petit Port at Le Havre (where it is convenient to unstep it), and stepped on return. This is by far the best idea for any sailing yacht intending to stay in the inland waterways, for the mast and rigging are always in the way on deck and the overhang of the mast can be a nuisance as already mentioned. Regular visitors to the inland waterways would be best suited with a motor cruiser.

Gas, paraffin and electrical appliances

Below deck, an inland waterway cruise calls for no special equipment. Bottled gas fittings in France are readily interchangeable with equipment supplied in the UK thanks to an adaptor that you can buy at any chandler or caravan store. The UK Calor bottles are not available in France where you use the Gaz containers widely available in shops and supermarkets. However, Camping Gaz is very expensive compared with 13 kg bottles of butane/propane, and empties can normally only be exchanged for full ones of the same brand. Empty Calor cylinders would be non-fare-paying passengers so plan accordingly.

If you happen to have paraffin appliances on board you will find that paraffin is widely available under the name of *Pétrole Supérieur*, from *Peintures, Drogueries*. Methylated spirit is obtainable from the same source, also from some food stores, and is known as *Alcool à Brûler*.

It is a good idea to have fire extinguishers strategically sited.

We used to talk about modest electrical equipment draining the batteries but now we have fridges, cookers, microwave ovens, music centres and a winking digital array of varied computer magic, all efficiently serviced and with silent generators in the background.

7 · Planning the cruise

Having decided upon your boat, the next step is to plan your cruise through the French canals.

The limits of your cruise will obviously depend upon the time that you have available and whether, in this time, you propose a return trip or a one-way trip, leaving your boat in France ready for your next cruising adventure (in which case you would either return by train or, more conveniently, in a hire care (see page 85).

You should apply to the French Government Tourist Office 178 Piccadilly, London, W1, for the current list of *chomages*, which shows which locks are closed for maintenance work and when; this maintenance work can extend throughout the summer months.

In addition to these lock closures for fixed repair periods some lock sections are closed on Sundays, some on Wednesdays. The first lock in any section will usually have the appropriate notice.

The following few extracts form a typical list of *chomages* will illustrate the necessity of consulting the current list before you plan your cruise:

Canal de Calais
Écluse d'Henuin (closed for 7 days from 22 June to 29 June)

Canal de la Somme
Écluses de Frise supérieure, de Froissy, de Montière et de Pont-Rémy (closed for 30 days from 30 June to 20 July)

Rivière de Marne
De l'écluse de Vandières à celle d'Azy (closed for 21 days from 1 to 22 July)

De l'écluse de Charly à celle de Lesches (closed for 21 days from 1 to 22 July)
De l'écluse de Lesches à celle de Neuilly sur Marne (closed for 15 days from 1 to 16 July)

Canal de la Marne au Rhin
De Vitry-le-François à Troussey (closed for 15 days from 7 to 22 July)
De Dombasle au bief de partage de Réchicourt aux petites portes du Lindres (closed for 15 days from 10 to 25 July)

Canal de Bourgogne
De Pont-Royal à St Jean-de-Losne (closed for 30 days from 1 May to 18 June)

Canal du Nivernais
De l'écluse de Loire No 35 à Cercy de la Tour (closed for 21 days from 9 to 30 August)
De Cercy la Tour à Sardy (closed for 26 days from 1 to 27 April)
De Sardy à Auxerre (closed for 20 days from 19 May to 8 June)

Rivière d'Yonne
D'Auxerre à Villevallier (closed for 22 days from 19 May to 10 June)
De Villevallier à Port-Renard (closed for 17 days from 22 May to 8 June)
De Port-Renard à Cannes (closed for 10 days from 22 May to 1 June)

These are a few examples from a list of sixty, but they will serve to illustrate the necessity of consulting the list of *chomages* before you plan your tour. A new list is available in March each year from the French Government Tourist Office.

A comprehensive list of all European waterways books and charts is available from Shepperton Swan Ltd, The Clock House, Upper Halliford, Shepperton, Middlesex TW17 8RU (Tel 0932 783319) or the Warsash Nautical Bookshop, 6 Dibles Road, Warsash, Southampton SO3 9HZ (Tel 04895 72384).

Waterway maps of France are also available from the Warsash Nautical Bookshop.

You will be planning your route, using the route map in conjunction with the route details and the appropriate Michelin map shown, noting the names of the towns that lie on or near the route of your proposed cruise. As already mentioned, the *Syndicat d'Initiative* at these towns will be pleased to send you details of items of interest or of any special event planned for the time that you will be there.

If you are going to need help with the Channel crossing to France it will also be necessary to arrange this with an experienced friend. You will obviously want the appropriate charts and your compass and other navigational aids should be checked so that you will be suitably prepared.

In previous editions of this book I have mentioned that cruising the French canals is free, but from 1 January 1992 boats cruising the French waterways have been required to pay a fee. It is fair that all waterway users should help to pay for their considerable upkeep, and no yachtsman is likely to object to the modest charges proposed. The Voies Navigables de France (VNF) is the independent authority set up by the French Government to manage the state waterway system.

The toll is due for any boat of 5 metres LOA or more, or for any boat with an engine developing 9.9 hp or more. On payment, a licence is issued for display on the boat.

The amount of the toll is based on the boat's surface area of length by beam, excluding pulpit or other 'outside' fittings. You can pay for one day, one week, one month, the season from 15 May to 31 October, or the whole year, per square metre, as follows:

Annual	Season	Month	Week	Day
50 F	30 F	20 F	5 F	1 F

A month can be any thirty day period.

Even as this new edition is finalized, the rates are changing, as one would expect. Another 45 day category has also been added. Apply in March to the French Government Tourist

Opposite and above: Very occasionally plans can go astray, as in May–June 1973, for instance, when the *batelier* went on strike and blocked the Seine at Rouen. Many yachts failed to get past the *batelier* barrier but many more were allowed through, some several times. Demands to pass, reminiscent of gunboat diplomacy, failed to open the strikers' hearts or barriers; charm, as ever, succeeded. The centre barges formed a 'gate' as shown above.

Office (FGTO) for a list of *chomages* and details of the VNF, enclosing a large SAE and you will receive them in April.

Over thirty payment centres are situated throughout France, at Calais, Dunkerque, Le Havre and Rouen, for instance, although not at all points of entry into the country. You can apply by post for a licence, giving name and address, name of boat, overall length and beam, registration number or series number, desired duration of licence and corresponding dates of validity to: Libraire VNF, 2 bd de Latour-Maubourg, 75343 PARIS CEDEX 07.

8 · In the waterways of France

This eighth edition of my book heralds a momentous change in the rules for taking your boat through the French canals. As I write, the new French rules are that, whoever happens to be at the helm (not necessarily the skipper) must be in possession of an appropriate certificate of competence, plus a copy of the CEVNI Rules, when in charge of any craft in the inland waterways of France.

Certificate C for craft up to 15 metres and up to 20 kph

Certificate PP for craft longer than 15 metres regardless of speed

Certificate S for craft faster than 20 kph regardless of length

You can satisfy the requirements of Certificate C by obtaining from the RYA the Helmsman's Overseas Certificate of Competence at a cost of £15 for non-members. If you are a member of the RYA (membership costs £15) the Certificate is issued free and you have the benefit of free, knowledgeable advice.

Certificates PP and S can only be obtained from the French Authorities at present, for which you will be examined in French. But does this mean that craft longer than 15 metres and faster than 20 kph can no longer cruise in the French canals unless they have these certificates? I am afraid that it does and this point has been forcefully put to the French authorities by the RYA. One would not imagine that it is a situation that will be allowed to continue, but the best advice is to keep in touch with the RYA at RYA House, Romsey Road, Eastleigh, Hampshire SO5 4YA (Tel 0703 629962 Fax 0703 629924).

If your boat has a mast it will be necessary to unstep it, and facilities for this exist at all entry ports (see p 42); there will also

Plenty of company . . .

. . . of all shapes and sizes. Over 300 cars on a 'Pusher' barge.

be fuel and water available, and it will be a sensible precaution to top up before setting off.

It will be an exciting moment when you set off on your inland cruise. If this happens to be a busy commercial waterway like the Seine, you will have plenty of interesting company of all shapes and sizes.

At first, until you get accustomed to it, the river traffic ahead will appear to be scattered all over your line of approach but, as in life, when you get up to them you will often find that the problems will have miraculously disappeared.

You will be the overtaken vessel.

Rules of the water-roads

The rule of the road is, of course, to keep to the right. When you get on to the shallower sections there is an exception to this rule; a heavily laden barge will have to follow the deep water channel whichever side of the waterway this takes him. If he comes over to 'your side' he will put out from the starboard side of his wheel-house a large blue board with a flashing white light at its centre and you then alter course to pass him on this side.

Whilst on the subject of passing it may be the moment to explain that when, later on, you come to the narrower canals you must slow down on meeting an oncoming barge and inch your way in towards the bank on your side as far as you dare. As his bow wave approaches you increase your speed and again when you are amidships of him, aiming back into the centre of the channel through the wash of his screw.

Right from the start you should keep a good look out for dredgers. They are usually held in their dredging position by a line to the bank and will be exhibiting a signal showing which side to pass. Sometimes dredgers are secured by lines to both banks and they will lower one of them into the water on your approach; but it is as well to look through the binoculars to be sure that they have seen you, not that your siren will be of much avail to announce your approach, for it would take an atomic explosion to compete with the racket of the dredging buckets.

If you see a barge displaying a red flag amidships it is an indication that he is turning in that direction and should not be overtaken on that side.

Difficult to pass – on the Marne . . .

Overtaking

It is likely that you will be the overtaken vessel most of the time, particularly on the wide waterways, and you will be overtaken without comment, just as you will overtake the odd slower craft that you come up on. Some yachts fit a rear mirror so that they can see what is coming up astern without turning round, but you do not really need this eye in the back of your head to the extent that you do in a car; boats and ships move relatively slower, and since it is likely that you will be interested enough to be looking all around you all the time, it will be a rare occasion that a craft will creep up on you unobserved. If you are in the way you will hear about it. If you keep well over to your side of the channel you will not attract attention.

In the narrower waterways where there is just room to pass, one is supposed to signal a request to overtake by hooting one long and one short if it is desired to pass to starboard and one long and two short if it is desired to pass to port. The answering signal to pass is one short to starboard and two short to port; four short means a refusal to let the overtaking vessel pass. This

...and on the Canal du Rhône au Rhin.

should not be construed as an outburst of bloody-mindedness, but simply that the skipper ahead can see a hazard that has not come into the view of the overtaking craft.

On some of the narrower canals, if you come up behind a barge going your way it is not likely that you will be able to pass him however much you toot. At each lock he will get ahead temporarily while the lock chamber is being refilled or re-emptied for you. It is foolish to allow yourself to become frustrated at being continually held up in this way. Far better to stop at some pleasant spot for sightseeing or shopping and thus allow the barge to get clear ahead. It may be that, by waiting, you will allow for the possibility of a barge coming from the opposite direction; then you will have all the locks 'set up' ready for you to enter (except in a few sections where the lock gates are always put one way after traffic has passed).

In case it may be wondered how barges going opposite ways can pass if it is impossible to pass when going the same way, the answer is that they squeeze past somehow. It takes so much longer to pass a barge when going the same way. You cannot

Narrow sections under bridges.

blame him for keeping going, and it is a hair raising experience to try to squeeze slowly by over his stern and bow wave with only inches to spare.

Bridges
When approaching bridges with a number of arches you will see signals on the bridges showing you which channel to take, as follows:

2 red horizontal bars with a white stripe between	*No entry* from the direction you are coming from
1 yellow diamond	*Two-way traffic*
2 yellow diamonds	*Entry* from your direction only (one-way traffic)

In the canals there are many narrow sections underneath bridges, and you will need to be ready to 'put your brakes on' urgently if a barge suddenly appears from round the corner ahead as you approach. Never attempt a race to the opening, for it is likely that you will be able to stop much quicker than the opposition. In going astern, as you will have to, be sure to go astern far enough, for the barge will sometimes clear the opening with maddening slowness; if you have gone ahead too soon it is an alarming experience to have the barge alongside you and no room ahead.

In fact, these encounters with barges are very rarely met, for it is usual to cruise all day long on the smaller canals without seeing more than two or three. But when you do meet them it is as well to be prepared.

Where 'traffic lights' are positioned at bridges, tunnels, locks, etc, the signal is:

Red	*Stop*
Green	*Go*
Red and Green	*Stand by*

Turning off

The channel that you are to follow is usually obvious, but not always so. The entrance to a lock might turn off quietly left or right, leaving what appears to be a splendid waterway ahead ... until you observe the spray haze rising up from the falling water of a weir. Near towns there are sometimes bridges busy with traffic that holds your attention, until it is diverted by a local citizen on the nearby bank afflicted, apparently, with St Vitus's Dance; you realize that he is only trying to attract your attention to dangers ahead. Going back you find that you have missed the proper turning.

Friendly relations

Although you can tie up anywhere you should avoid doing so near to locks because barges will want to wait or pass here and it is likely that they will be up earlier than you in the morning. No traffic moves on the majority of French waterways at night and it is a delight to tie up to trees, by some grassy bank, in the certain knowledge that your sleep is not going to be disturbed.

Avoid tying up near to locks.

I have heard 'bargees' (*bateliers*) and lock-keepers criticized as being unhelpful and unkind to yachtsmen, but I have never had this experience. Some people have a facility for rubbing everyone up the wrong way and they complain when the effect of their attitude rebounds on them. In life generally, scowls are traded for scowls and smiles for smiles; the French canals are no exception.

Go through the inland waterways determined to have an enjoyable cruise and everyone you meet will help you to achieve it.

9 · Locks

Times of opening

1 to 15 October	6.30 am to 6.30 pm
16 to 31 October	7.00 am to 6.00 pm
1 November to 31 January	7.30 am to 5.30 pm
February	7.30 am to 6.30 pm
1 to 15 March	7.00 am to 7.00 pm
16 March to 30 September	6.30 am to 7.30 pm
(Only a few waterways are worked all night)	
Rhône locks	5.00 am to 9.00 pm

These times of opening vary from one waterway to another; the table above is a guide only. For more detail you should consult the appropriate *Carte Guide*. Some canals, eg the Canal de Bourgogne and Canal du Midi are generally closed in the winter nowadays since there is no longer any commercial traffic on them.

What to expect

A certain competence in handling a boat is necessary in order to make the trip through the canals, and no special skill is needed to go in and out of locks. As for being worried about locks simply because of their size, the biggest of all, the Bollène, raises or lowers you in its 25 m (82 ft) cathedral-like chamber without a ripple. By comparison, a lock-keeper 'cowboy' (rare indeed), can cause discomfort by changing a 1.50 m (5 ft) level too quickly if you are not secured properly.

Locks vary in size and operation according to the traffic carried. Some locks have a gate in the centre, so that it can be a half-size or a full-size lock according to the traffic. Busy waterway sections have big locks, often automatically operated. More and more automatically controlled locks are now triggered by radar, which recognises the approach of your craft. If it fails to do so, go ashore and use the lock telephone which is a direct line to help. Some automatic locks need to be operated yourself.

The quieter country sections have small single locks, manually operated by the lock-keeper or, more usually, by his wife assisted by a crew member of the boat passing through.

Entering the French waterways from England, the commercial size locks will be the first to be encountered, and it may therefore be as well to consider the big locks first; also ascending locks, since these will need to be dealt with before the descending.

Ascending your first lock

Imagine that you are approaching your first lock. Barges will be waiting their turn to enter, quite often more barges than the lock will accommodate; some barges will be secured to the bank, others drifting in the waterway, others coming up fast astern. All will be leaving a way clear for the 'other way' barges to come out of the lock (we are assuming that our first lock is filling from the opposite direction as we approach).

The invariable rule for pleasure craft is to keep out of the way of all commercial craft, displaying to them 'after you' politeness which they will appreciate. Seek no preference over a barge because you arrived at the lock before him.

At the same time, try to satisfy yourself that the waiting barges are, in fact, waiting for the lock and not just waiting. In some of the industrial areas, barges, three and four deep, secure to quays waiting for work. These quays may be just before a lock, and you would have a long wait if you decided to defer to some of them. Even barges that you are following may decide to 'park'. If you have any doubt about such a situation always enquire, in French or sign language, by going alongside the nearest occupied barge. In a wide waterway there can be no harm in going ahead to have a look at the lock, returning to a suitable station having done so. In a narrow waterway this will not be wise as the waiting barges may be queuing to enter a one-way section or traffic-light-controlled tunnel.

If you can see the lock ahead you will be able to judge how

long you will have to wait to enter. Barges in the lock going your way will mean a long wait; or if the lock is just filling with barges from the opposite direction it will be best for you to secure.

Do not assume that because a barge is secured to the bank there will be sufficient water for you alongside the bank unless the barge is deeply laden. In any case it will usually be more convenient for you to go alongside a barge that is tied up to the bank; if the *batelier* is in view, a raised warp and eyebrow accompanied by a smile will be sufficient to obtain his approval. If he is not in view simply secure to the bitts on his deck. Your crew will have a warp ready to loop over the bitts, and the *batelier* may even help you to secure. This is an occasion when your stock of sweets (brought specially for the purpose) will be brought out if you see any children on the barge.

Secure to the barge in such a manner that you can instantly cast off. Keep a lookout for any new arrival coming up astern and vacate your place alongside if there appears to be nowhere

'Other Way' traffic will come streaming out.

Some locks are operated . . .

else for the newcomer to secure, particularly if he is a big or
double barge.

These gestures are noted and appreciated; some of the barges
waiting in your company at this lock may be in your company
for the rest of the day through other locks when you may need
them.

When the lock opens, the 'other way' traffic will come
streaming out. If the waterway is wide enough for you to stay
well clear of this oncoming traffic, do so; in narrow waterways
remain secured to the bank fore and aft until it has passed or it
will suck you in towards it as it goes by. As soon as it has all
passed by, let go and move out of the way of the barges going in.
Stay to one side as near to the lock as convenient.

The lock-keeper's directions will echo over the water from his
loudspeaker, but do not be concerned if you cannot understand
what he is saying. It is unlikely that a pleasure craft would be
directed into the lock first so you will have time to watch the
barges.

The barges move forward as directed, and where directed if
the lock has more than one chamber, tucking themselves in
alongside each other. As the lock space is taken up you stand up

...from
control
towers.

nearer, out of the way to one side, ready to move ahead. 'After you' politeness is not discarded but the time approaches when barges waiting with you will not be able to get into the space left and you will.

At this time it may be that the loudspeaker will call you forward; it may be that you will not understand what the loudspeaker voice is saying. It is then likely that from the waiting barges (impressed by your politeness) will appear much shouting and waving urging you forward.

If there is no loudspeaker it is simply a question of judging when no more barges can be taken in but you can; or perhaps the last barge is seen thrashing astern, unable to squeeze in.

You move ahead smartly; one lock gate will probably be closing as you approach, perhaps both. As you prepare to nose inside, a lock-keeper may indicate where he wants you to lie

Secured to a barge in a lock only half full of barges.

but, more probably, there will be only one obvious space available.

Your foredeck hand should have a coiled rope in hand ready to throw in case the lock-keeper shows any interest in receiving it and assuming that he is near. It is probable that he will be if the lock gates are manually operated. Some of the bigger locks and all of the huge ones are operated by the remote control of a lock-keeper in a control tower. The really big locks have vast steel shutters that rise up and down instead of gates.

The lock sides will be too high for you to climb. It is not likely that there will be iron rungs set in the lock wall just where you are. If the lock-keeper holds out his hand for your warp he will appreciate receiving it accurately thrown, first time. When ropes have become soggy bundles of knitting that fall short of the lock-keeper's outstretched hand he is liable to walk away. If he receives your line he will take it round a bollard (out of your vision since you are 'down below') and throw the end back down to you if it is long enough.

Movable bollards
slide up and
down the walls
in deep locks.

If the lock-keeper does not appear to take your line, you secure to a barge; in the space left for you it may not be a question of selecting one, for the last in will be the only one that you can get at to secure.

His decks may be cleaner than yours so try not to dirty them; his sides most certainly will not be, so have your fenders out over the side as protection.

Lock with sloping sides.

Made to measure.

Whilst securing, keep your eye on the lock gates closing behind you to make sure that your stern has not drifted back into them.

Soon after the gates close, the water level will begin to rise. If you are secured to one of the lock bollards you must take up on your rope as you rise, to keep your station; secured to a barge you have no worry in this respect.

An object
lesson . . .

. . . in relaxed
control.

As you rise up above the lock wall it is wise to detach, if you are secured to a barge, and push off to secure to a bollard on the lock. All the barges in the lock will be getting ready to move out as soon as the gates ahead open; when their screws start turning you will need to be secured. The swirling water will create no problem if you are tied to a bollard.

Allow all the barges to go on ahead before you let go. You may see them tossing something to the lock-keeper (stationed judiciously) as they leave. It is not necessary for a pleasure craft to consider tipping unless some very special service has been rendered.

Having successfully negotiated your first lock you realize that there was nothing to worry about after all.

Securing lines

In very deep, large, locks there are set in the lock walls, movable bollards that slide up and down with you so that there is no need to adjust your ropes as the water level changes. Or sometimes, in smaller locks, the lock-keeper of a deep lock will reach down a long pole with a hook on the end to take your

Lock open in your favour.

Winding up the sluice handles . . .

. . . to let the
water in.

warp. Some yachts carry such poles, with hooks on the end, for passing warps to lock-keepers and for reaching around bollards.

Not all locks have straight sides; where they are sloping, 'V' shaped, it is slightly more difficult to get a line ashore, and instead of trying to do so it will be easier to secure to a barge if one is available. (Some locks have one side sloping and one straight.)

Smaller locks

However, small locks will be the ones most frequently encountered. Since they fit the type of barge using them like a glove, there is no question of sharing these locks with a barge. See the series of photographs (p 66–67) showing how snugly the barge *Malvine* fits into the lock; 'made for it' one might say, as indeed the barges are. Incidentally, the lady 'driver' of *Malvine* is an object lesson in relaxed control as she manoeuvres her huge charge through the lock.

The smaller locks are on the waterways with little traffic, and it is usual to go for a whole day without meeting more than two or three barges.

Two or three yachts can be accommodated in the smaller locks, and the lock routine can then be shared between crews.

On approaching a small lock, if the gates are closed against you and no one is in view, a toot on your siren/hooter will usually bring someone from the lock house to start opening one gate for you. Whether anyone appears or not, nose your craft into the bank and put a crew member ashore, to find the lock-keeper, if necessary, and to open the other gate. If the beam of your boat allows you to enter through one opened gate, your crew member will go up the lock ladder once inside.

Should it be lunch time, this will be the moment to have your own lunch, too. Many lock-keepers like to have their lunch undisturbed, and who can blame them?

Obviously the gates will not be opened for you until the water in the lock chamber is equalized on your level.

If, on approaching, the lock gates are open, look to see whether the iron rung ladder is set in the right or left wall. They are situated fairly constantly, all right or all left, for long sections of locks at a time, and only appear to change when you get too confident in your anticipation.

Circular lock. It is impossible to keep all of the boat alongside. Watch for
occasional sluices causing cross currents.

Nose your craft up to the ladder so that your crew can step
off on to it carrying a suitable length of attached (to the boat)
bow warp coiled over his or her shoulder like a mountain
climber. The crew should get into the habit of gaining the quay
quickly and allowing for the pull on the warp once the boat
starts moving into the lock. Move on into the lock, and instruct
the crew to take a turn round a bollard and throw the end of the
warp back down to you. If your crew is already ashore to open
the gate, you will need to have your warp ready coiled to throw
and to stand by for its return. Secure aft and be ready to take up
as the water rises.

The lock-keeper will close one gate behind you, and if the
second gate has been opened your crew will close that. They
will then walk up to the gates ahead and wind up the sluice
handles to let the water in.

When the lock water level is equalized, the lock-keeper and
your crew will wind open the forward gates; you toss your warp
from the bollard (having taken up on it the whole time that the
water was coming into the lock), your crew steps on board, and
you wave goodbye to the lock-keeper.

Looking
down a
flight of
seven
staircase locks.

The gate ahead becomes the gate behind as you move forward.

Lock types

There are many different types of locks: large, small, straight-sided, sloping, rectangular, circular, but they all follow the same pattern in the same waterway section.

Staircase locks are a series of locks joined together, the inside lock gates of the first lock chamber being the outside lock gates of the next and so on. When you are going through staircase locks, having put your crew ashore at the first one as already described, you move out of one lock into the next one, your crew remaining ashore to carry your warp up (or down) the staircase.

In cases where there are no facilities to put your crew ashore and there appears to be special difficulty in getting a warp ashore without help, it will invariably be found that the necessary help is readily available to greet you. It is sometimes easy to forget that one is not the first to pass that way.

Crew waiting to rejoin after lock 'duty'.

Variety and interest. From a country lock to ...

(opposite) ... the Bollène.

Descending locks

So far, the procedure for ascending has been outlined.
Descending is easier in that you enter the lock at quay level and
can reach out to loop your warp over a bollard. But if, on
approach, the gates are closed against you it will be appreciated
(by the lock-keeper) if you put your crew ashore to open the
second gate should your boat be unable to fit through the space
left by the gate opened by the lock-keeper. (Incidentally,
whether ascending or descending, if you do not put crew ashore
to help the lock-keeper he will, of course, do it all himself—in
time.)

Your crew and the lock-keeper walk ahead to the forward
gates to open the sluices. It is now of the utmost importance to
ensure that your warp is not secured both ends on board. If
they are, the rope will tighten up as you are lowered in the lock,

the deck fitting to which it is attached will be pulled out; or the rope will break; or your boat will be left hanging on the lock wall.

But I am sorry to say that this happens to the best of us; in fact it is easy enough to be diverted at that vital moment when the level of water is going down in the lock chamber and your warp is coming up taut. Kettles always whistle at such moments, and you just pop into the cabin to turn the heat off; or you may be searching in the cabin for something that a comment by the lock-keeper has brought to your mind.

Your turn round your cleat may be impossible to undo when it comes under considerable strain. If you are faced with this situation, shout immediately to have the sluices closed; it may then be necessary to let in some water again (from the other end of the lock, of course) to take off the strain and get your warp free.

Locks with sloping sides obviously need a special routine, for when descending in them your hull will quickly make contact with the sloping lock wall. If you have bilge keels they will be caught in the uneven stonework of the wall and your boat will heel over as the water level falls away. Should this happen you must again shout for the sluices to be closed; if you then cannot push yourself free, the lock must be refilled until you can.

A simple routine to avoid these problems in descending sloping locks is to position yourself amidships holding the boat-hook and/or a long pole to push your boat away from the lock wall as you descend. You will need to have the free end of your warp in your hands as well, gently pulling on the warp (which will be around a bollard ashore) and pushing on the boat-hook to maintain position. If you have sufficient crew to 'pole off' at either end of the boat, so much the better.

Another point to watch in descending is that you are far enough forward in the lock (away from the gates you have entered) to avoid the possibility of your rudder lodging on the shelf or step just inside the lock.

When you are down to the required water level, your warp is pulled back on board; for this reason the warp is passed round the bollard and not tied to it.

Whether in sloping or straight-sided locks you are now 'low

down' and your crew is 'high up' ashore. If there are iron rungs set in the lock wall your crew will come down them to you. Sometimes, in place of rungs in the lock wall, there are steps at the end of the lock, and your crew can rejoin the boat from there.

In ascending locks the chamber will obviously be filled by water flowing in from ahead of you and often a bow warp only would suffice to secure you; in descending locks, with the flow going past from astern of you, a stern warp would often suffice. But it is wise to make a habit of securing fore and aft at all times; a single warp around one bollard ashore will do. You will then be safeguarded against swirls and eddies. If you swing out of line, look to your helm. Your boat will steer in the moving water filling or emptying the lock and the position of your rudder is clearly of great importance.

On some waterways, the Saône and Rhône, for instance, you can alert the lock-keeper to your arrival, which helps sometimes.

10 · Cost of living, shopping and stores

At the present rate of exchange (1994) there are approximately 8 francs to the pound.

One of the greatest joys, of course, is the cheapness of the best wine in the world and many other drinks. *Vin Ordinaire* seems to be available in supermarkets everywhere. There are many different brands so do not be put off if you do not fancy the first one you try. VDQS wines cost from 80p upwards a bottle and *Appellation Contrôlée* wines from £1. At these prices you have a wonderful opportunity to experiment.

Living is no dearer in France than it is in England at the present time and the choice and arrangement of French food for sale generally has always been preferred by a lot of people. Shopping in France should be a joyful experience and I feel sorry for those so 'dull of soul' that they find it a bore.

Most holidaymakers are obliged to eat out, which is obviously more expensive than eating at home; but the yachtsman in France has with him his cruising home so that he can appreciate the delight of French shops, supermarkets and open markets.

The coffee and snack habit is expensive in any country. You get the best selection of *prix fixe* meals in France, also they will be beautifully presented and served long after the 'chef's gone home' time in Britain.

It should be obvious that bacon and eggs for breakfast are as relatively expensive in France as *croissants* are in England. Holidaymakers who insist upon continuing English eating habits when abroad are usually the loudest to complain about the cost of living.

When people are so insistent that the cost of living is prohibitive in France I can never understand how they imagine that the ordinary French people live; for the average wage there is not very high and yet one sees very few bodies lying around on the pavements in an emaciated condition. For myself, I do not complain about the cost of butter in a country where one can buy a bottle of *Appellation Contrôlée* wine for only a little over £1.

Local produce

Every town and village seems to have its charming little market where vegetables, eggs, and chickens are brought in fresh from the country and cost no more than they do in the UK, if as much. The chickens are not always dressed, it is true, and sometimes your purchase is handed to you alive, trussed by the feet, in which case you will have a most interesting cycle ride in getting it back to the boat. And once on board it is likely that your meal will be long deferred.

Lock-keepers in the country sections sometimes have eggs and vegetables to sell. Often there are a variety of shops near locks. The most constant shopping need is for bread and milk, of course, which costs much the same as it does in the UK. You can buy bread every day including Sundays and holidays; if one *boulangerie* is closed it is likely that there will be another one open nearby.

A longish lunch period is usual for all shops, but they stay open until quite late in the evening. Many shops close on Mondays, but the village store type of shop seems to be open for long hours every day and often on Sundays and holidays.

Provisions from home

Long-life milk (*lait au longue conservation*) should always be carried for emergencies. In fact, you can keep your cost of living down in France by taking with you as many cans of food as your storage space will hold. Meat is relatively dear in France, so why not take with you a large selection of canned varieties; sausages, as we know them, are virtually unobtainable, so that if you are partial to the good old English 'banger' you should take what you can with you. Butter is dear, but can you tell margarine from butter? Jams and marmalades are also expensive in France, so that your stores should include these together with café size tins of coffee, milk drinks and a really large box of tea bags. You cannot buy the bacon that you are accustomed to in England, but will probably prefer to eat a French breakfast when in France. Although there are hundreds of different cheeses made in France, few of them are cheap.

Buying fuel

The main item of shopping for your boat will be fuel. Petrol costs more than diesel fuel in France.

Wherever there are cars and trucks there will always be fuel stations somewhere, but if you allow your fuel tanks to run low, that will surely be the time when you are a long way from a fuel station. Waterside diesel points are increasing, but you should always top up when opportunity offers. If you decide to take a bicycle it will provide wheels for your heavy fuel loads. So will a folding shopping trolley.

Calor Gas fittings are not necessarily interchangeable with Continental Butane Gas fittings, but there is an adapter available to convert Calor Gas fittings for use with Camping Gaz which is widely available, although rather expensive.

Shopping vocabulary

apple – *pomme*
apricot – *abricot*
artichoke – *artichaut*
asparagus – *asperges*
bacon – *lard*
baker – *boulangerie*
banana – *banane*
beef – *boeuf*
beefsteak – *bifteck*
  (well done – *bien cuit*;
  medium – *à point*;
  rare – *saignant*)
beer – *bière*
beetroot – *betterave*
blackcurrant – *cassis*
bread – *pain*

broccoli – *brocoli*
Brussels sprouts –
  choux de Bruxelles
butcher – *boucherie*
butter – *beurre*
cabbage – *chou*
can opener – *ouvre-boîte*
carrot – *carrotte*
cauliflower –
  choufleur
celery – *céleri*
cheese – *fromage*
chemist – *pharmacie*
cherries – *cerises*
chicken – *poulet*
chop – *côte*

cocoa – *cacao*
cod – *morue*
coffee – *café*
confectioners –
  confiserie
crab – *crabe*
cream – *crème*
cucumber –
  concombre
cutlets – *côtelettes*
duck – *canard*
egg – *oeuf*
figs – *figues*
fish – *poisson*
fishmonger –
  poissonnerie
flour – *farine*

French beans – *haricots verts*
frogs – *grenouilles*
fruit – *fruit*
fruit shop – *fruiterie*
grape – *raisin*
grapefruit – *pamplemousse*
grocer – *épicerie*
haddock – *eglefin*
hake – *colin*
halibut – *flétan*
ham – *jambon*
herring – *hareng*
honey – *miel*
ice – *glace*
jam – *confiture*
kidney beans – *flageolets*
kidneys – *rognons*
lamb – *agneau*
lark – *alouette*
lemon – *citron*
lettuce – *laitue*
liver – *foie* (beef liver – *foie de boeuf*; calves' liver – *foie de veau*; lambs' liver – *foie d'agneau*)
lobster – *homard*

mackerel – *maquereau*
margarine – *margarine*
marrow – *moelle*
meat – *viande*
milk – *lait*
mushrooms – *champignons*
mussels – *moules*
mustard – *moutarde*
mutton – *mouton*
oil – *huile*
olive – *olive*
onion – *oignon*
orange – *orange*
oysters – *huîtres*
parsnip – *panais*
pastry shop – *pâtisserie*
peach – *pêche*
pear – *poire*
peas – *pois*
pineapple – *ananas*
plaice – *carrelet* or *plie*
plum – *prune*
pork – *porc*
potato – *pomme de terre*

prawns – *bouquets* or *crevettes*
rabbit – *lapin*
raspberry – *framboise*
rhubarb – *rhubarbe*
salmon – *saumon*
salt – *sel*
sausages – *saucissons*
slice – *tranche*
snails – *escargots*
sole – *sole*
soup – *potage*
spaghetti – *spaghetti*
spinach – *épinards*
strawberry – *fraise*
sugar – *sucre*
sweetbreads – *ris de veau*
tart – *tarte*
tea – *thé*
thrush – *grive*
tin – *boîte*
tomato – *tomate*
tripe – *tripes*
trout – *truite*
turbot – *turbot*
turnip – *navets*
veal – *veau*
vinegar – *vinaigre*
water – *eau*

Engine breakdowns

If you are unfortunate enough to have an engine breakdown you will find that the average French mechanic is quite resourceful in dealing with purely motor departments of your engine; as far as the marine department is concerned there are marine engineers at many of the points where barges gather. To

Petrol pumps alongside, Auxerre.

take a kit of spares is a reasonable precaution, for it usually ensures that the parts you have duplicated will keep running satisfactorily.

Mechanical vocabulary

acid – *acide*
armature – *armature*
battery, to top – *reniveler la batterie*
bolt – *boulon*
carburettor – *carburateur*
choke – *starter*
diesel – *diesel*
diesel fuel – *gas-oil*
dipstick – *réglette-jauge*

distributor – *distributeur*
distributor head – *distributeur de courant*
dynamo – *dynamo*
engine – *moteur*
fill up – *faire le plein*
fuel tank – *réservoir d'essence* (or *gas-oil*)
insulating tape – *chatterton*

jet – *gicleur*
nut – *écrou*
oil – *huile*
petrol – *essence*
screw – *vis*
screwdriver – *tournevis*
self-starter – *démarreur*
spanner, adjustable – *clé à molette*
washer – *rondelle*
water – *eau*

11 · Weather and miscellaneous items of interest

Weather

Spring and summer are the best times to cruise in the French canals, but some are closed for varying periods from May to September, and the list of *chomages* should be consulted as already explained. It seems that the experienced French canal-cruising folk prefer to go in April, May, or June. It is well known that all France is on holiday during July and August, not that this means crowded cruising, for the Frenchman is strangely disinterested in using his beautiful waterways; but the holiday crowds would make demands on the facilities ashore. Up to March there is likely to be flooding, when some weirs are opened to navigation and locks are not then used. From September there is likely to be drought; for this latter reason navigation is sometimes impossible in September, October, and November. Therefore, for any proposed cruise outside the months of April to August it would be more than ever necessary to make advance enquiries through the local canal authority offices in France regarding the possibility of completing the journey. Even then, conditions can change from day to day. The seasonal climate of France is not all that much different from our own except, perhaps, for the winter-protected Côte d'Azur. Marseille in December can be as cold as London; and from December, incidentally, the French canals can be ice-bound.

French weather reports can be obtained through the various motor organizations. A fall in barometric pressure as one climbs lock by lock need not cause alarm and is to be expected.

Public holidays in France

New Year's Day, Easter Monday, 1 May, Ascension Day,

Whit Monday, 14 July (Bastille Day), 15 August, 1 November, 11 November, 25 December.

Banks close on these public holidays, also all day on Saturdays (and Sundays, needless to say); on weekdays they are open from 9 am to 4 pm, many closing for an hour or so at lunch time.

Cruiser hire

There are many hire cruisers on the inland waterways of France and the popularity of this type of holiday grows every year. In a way – apart from considering the desirability or otherwise of allowing learners on the waterways – it provides proof that you do not need to be an experienced sailor to embark on a voyage of this nature. The owners of such hire craft would not risk their valuable fleets nor would insurers insure them. Obviously

Canals can be ice-bound from December.

it is preferable to have nautical experience to cruise your craft in the inland waterways – and essential to get it there.

In addition to the hire cruisers that you 'drive yourself' there are passenger-carrying cruise ships, often converted barges, providing luxury travel and sometimes luxury food. We have met them on the Marne, Seine, Yonne and in the Burgundy, Centre, Nivernais, Loing, Briare and Loire Canals. (Such pampered cruising does not prepare for a waterway life in your own boat, however.) We have been interested to note that many of the passenger-carrying cruise ships have been operated by British owners who have thus discovered an agreeable way of being paid to cruise the inland waterways of France.

There are charter cruisers in many areas of France now, and a list of the many hire cruisers available may be obtained from the French Government Tourist Office in London, who will send you regional catalogues.

Hire cars
It is quite possible to leave your boat in France so that you can continue your cruise when next you have time available. If you can make it convenient to leave your boat at a place where 'drive-yourself' hire cars are available, you will be able to bring off your personal gear with the minimum of inconvenience. Hertz and Avis cars are available at many towns throughout France; wherever you hire them from, you can drive them to Le Havre or any other Channel port and leave them there.

Mail
Can be sent to you c/o *poste restante* at any town and is reliable. A small charge is made on collection of letters.

Cats and dogs
Cats and dogs can be brought into France provided that they have either:
● A certificate of origin and health, dated not earlier than three days before the animals' journey, stating that it comes from a country where there has been no epidemic of rabies for three years and that it has spent at least six months in that country, or has been there since birth.

● A certificate of anti-rabies vaccination stating that the vaccination was given with a vaccine officially administered more than one month and less than six months before entry into France.

Puppies less than three months old and kittens less than six months old may be taken into France upon production of a veterinary certificate confirming age.

Health precautions

If you are planning to be abroad for a long time it can be an expensive business fixing up Travel Insurance with an insurance

The River Marne.

Weights and measures

litres	gals		kms	miles		kgs	lbs
1 =	0.22		1 =	0.62		0.453 =	1
2 =	0.44		2 =	1.24		0.907 =	2
3 =	0.66		3 =	1.86		1.360 =	3
4 =	0.88		4 =	2.48		1.814 =	4
5 =	1.10		5 =	3.11		2.268 =	5
6 =	1.32		6 =	3.73		2.721 =	6
7 =	1.54		7 =	4.35		3.175 =	7
8 =	1.76		8 =	4.97		3.628 =	8
9 =	1.98		9 =	5.59		4.082 =	9
10 =	2.20		10 =	6.21		4.535 =	10
15 =	3.30		15 =	9.32			
20 =	4.40		20 =	12.43			
30 =	6.60		30 =	18.64			
40 =	8.80		40 =	24.85			
50 =	11.00		50 =	31.07			
100 =	22.00		100 =	62.14			

company. Whether or not this is arranged, UK citizens should go to their local Department of Health and Social Security for a Form E111 which is a Certificate of Entitlement to Benefits in Kind during a stay in a Member State under the European Communities Social Security Regulations.

I have reason to be grateful for this scheme since I was suddenly laid low when we were moored in the middle of Le Havre harbour. In no time at all a speedy craft was alongside with attendants in wet suits plus a charming lady doctor; an ambulance was waiting on the quay and I was being dealt with in a super-efficient hospital within the hour. Having been restored to health with great kindness and skill I can testify that the French medical authorities honour the reciprocal health agreement in splendid and charming fashion. I can only hope that we do as well for French nationals in need.

Canals *do* close for repairs. The photographs illustrate why you must obtain a list of *chomages* from the French Government Tourist office before you go.

12 · Route details section

Limits of length and breadth

(height above waterline and draft are shown in metres above each route)

River/Canal	Length m	Breadth m
River Seine – from Rouen to Corbeil	141.00	11.60
Canals linking Paris with Lyon via Burgundy	38.50	5.00
Canals linking Paris with Lyon via Nevers and the Bourbonnais	38.50	5.00
Canals linking Paris with Lyon via the River Marne	38.50	5.00
Canals linking Paris with Northern France	38.50	5.00
Canals linking Paris with Belgium	38.50	5.00
Canals linking Paris with Strasbourg	38.50	5.00
Canal de la Marne à la Saône	38.50	5.00
Canal du Rhône au Rhin	33.70	5.10
Canal du Midi	30.00	5.25
Canal latéral à la Garonne	30.00	5.80
Nantes–Redon–Rennes–St Malo	26.00	4.50

Berry au Bac. Canal latéral à l'Aisne. Barge with wheelhouse folded down.

Route 1
Agde to Royan

Distance: **598 km (371 M)**   Number of locks: **140**   Minimum height above water: **3.47 m**
Minimum depth of water: **1.45 m**

The future of the Canal du Midi has been in doubt. Readers may recall that the section
between Carcassonne and Toulouse was closed for two years prior to 1991 due to water
shortage, but the problems have now been resolved.

Navigations	Km	Locks	Towns and Villages	Michelin Map No
ETANG DU THAU			Sète	83
	19		Marseillan	83
CANAL DU MIDI	3			
		3		
	8		Agde (pop: 13 000). Old seaport and fishing port. 12th C church, was a cathedral. Museum, local folklore.	83
		5		
	24		Béziers (pop: 90 000). Centre of Hérault and Aude wine regions; in particular the town is associated with the red wine known locally as *Gros Rouge*. It is said that blancmange was invented here. Churches: St Aphrodise, 11th–15th C; Madeleine, originally Romanesque. Museums: pictures, Greek vases, local interest and the wine trade. Garden of poets.	83
(Water slope)				
Tunnel		1		
	13		Poilhes Nearby is Oppidum d'Ensérune, the only fully excavated pre-Roman city in France.	83
	6		Capestang Quay, cruiser line.	83
LEFT *Canal to La Nouvelle. See Route 1A*	21 13		Roubia Pleasant mooring, few shops.	83

Navigations	Km	Locks	Towns and Villages	Michelin Map No
CANAL DU MIDI		5		
	13		**La Redorte** Quay and shops.	83
		4		
	13		**Marseillette** Mooring and shops.	83
		1		
	10		**Trebes** Pleasant shops.	83
		6		
	11		**Carcassonne** (pop: 41 000). Outstanding example of fortified medieval town with double ramparts restored 19th C. Enclosed city fortress with 54 towers, but town has expanded beyond. Churches: St Vincent, 14th C; St Michael, 13th C. The wine-growing area of Corbières is situated in the foothills of the Pyrenees with Carcassonne in the North West and the Mediterranean in the East. It is the largest producer of VDQS wines in France and has one wine, Fitou, of *Appellation Contrôlée*. Strong red wines with pleasant	83

Carcassonne

Navigations	Km	Locks	Towns and Villages	Michelin Map No
CANAL DU MIDI			bouquet are mainly produced. Splendid quay and facilities (see photo).	
		4		
	13		**Villesequelande** Attractive quay.	83
		1		
	11		**Bram** Quay and shops.	82
		11		
	13		**Castelnaudary** (pop: 10 000). Well known for *cassoulet*, a form of stew, and for its cooking generally. 14th C church of St Michel. Convenient quays, access to shops. Hire cruiser base.	82
			Port Lauragais Marina, near autoroute service station.	82
		4		
	14		**Gardouch** Quay, village.	82
		5		
	11		**Montgiscard** Interesting shops.	82
		2		
	13		**Port Sud** Marina, services, shops, restaurant.	82
		3		
	1		**Ramonville** Industrial basin.	82
	7		**Port Saint-Sauveur** Basin.	82
	21		**Toulouse** (pop: 354 000). Fourth largest city in France. Cultural and business centre. University established here over 700 years ago. Many old churches and fine houses. Museums: Delacroix, Corot, Ingrès, Poussin, Toulouse-Lautrec. Toulouse cathedral is said to be the most complete romanesque church in France. Hire cruiser base. All facilities. Port de l'embouchure.	82
		6		

Navigations	Km	Locks	Towns and Villages	Michelin Map No
CANAL LATERAL A LA GARONNE	5			
		2		
	6		**Fenouillet**	82
		4		
	8		**St Jory**	82
		3		
	11		**Grissolles**	82
	6		**Dieupentale** Quay.	82
		1		
RIGHT *into Canal to Montauban*	16		**Montauban** (pop: 53 000). Capital of the department of Tarn-et-Garonne. Once a fortress. Famous bridge (the Tarn bridge). Church: St Jacques, 14th C. Ingrès Museum: mainly pictures and drawing of Ingrès, also Delacroix, Poussin.	82
			Montech Water slope is of interest.	82, 79
		8		
	13		**Castelsarrasin** Good moorings and shops.	79
		7		
	8		**Moissac** (pop: 11 500). Peaceful old town. Good market. Pleasant stop. Basin.	79
		4		
	16		**Valence d'Agen** Quay.	79
		1		
	6		**Lamagistere** Quay.	79
		2		
	19		**Agen** (pop: 35 000). Capital of Lot-et-Garonne. Narrow streets in the old quarter giving way to broad boulevards. Fashionable shops. The name of Agen is associated with prunes; try the prune preserve. St Caprais Cathedral, 11th–16th C; Notre Dame, 13th C; St Hillaire, 15th C. Museum: ceramics, furniture, tapestries, paintings, including Goya's self portrait; Gallo-Roman antiquities. Between Agen and Bayonne is the Region of Armagnac	79
Junction Canalized River Baise to River Lot, 65 km, 14 locks reopened for navigation in 1990				

Navigations	Km	Locks	Towns and Villages	Michelin Map No
CANAL LATERAL A LA GARONNE			brandy. It is the oldest of French brandies prepared by slow continuous distillation from Gascon Picpoult grapes, Bas-Armagnac (black Armagnac) brandies are particularly sought after. The nearest distillery is at Condom, and visitors are welcome to look around. Splendid yachting facilities, water, fuel, harbour.	
		7		
	27		**Buzet** Excellent shopping facilities. Harbour.	79
	3		**Damazan** Good shops nearby. Harbour.	79
		2		
	6		**Tonneins** Quay.	79
		1		
	6		**Le Mas d'Agenais** Quay.	79
		4		
	18		**Meilhan** Basin.	79
		6		
RIVER GARONNE	18		**Castets-en-Dorthe** Basin.	79
	7		**Langon** A small area here produces Sauternes and Barsac, the best sweet wines in the world. Only white wines are produced here and they are naturally sweet. In this region the grapes are picked when they are over-ripe and each grape is picked individually. Thus each grape contains a large amount of sugar which gives the natural sweetness for which these wines are famous.	79, 71
	6		**Barsac** Quay.	79, 71
	4		**Cadillac** Quay.	79, 71
	3		**Podensac** Quay. Village.	79, 71
	4		**Lestiac** Quay.	79, 71

Navigations	Km	Locks	Towns and Villages	Michelin Map No
RIVER GARONNE	6		**Portets** Quay.	79, 71
	6		**Cambes** Quay.	79, 71
	5		**Bordeaux** (pop: 600 000). Principal port, particularly for wine, and one of the most important industrial and tourist centres. Fifth largest city in France; centre of the most famous wine growing area in the world. Grand Théâtre, 1776–80. St Andre Cathedral, 11th C; St Seurin, 12–15th C; Palais Gallien, 18th C. Remains of Roman amphitheatre. Museum: notable paintings, sculpture, and maritime. Real Bordeaux wine only comes from Bordeaux; the greater part of the annual Bordeaux crop is offered under district names and wine from the best vineyards – less than 10 per cent of the total – is usually sold under the name of the château of origin. Bordeaux Rouge, a rather light wine, covers all Bordeaux wines not sold under another district name. Visits to vineyards, cellars, also tasting can be arranged; the *Syndicat d'Initiative* will provide latest information. East of Bordeaux is St Emilion, a vineyard of repute in Roman times. The region of St Emilion produces not only St Emilion itself, but also wines whose names are made up of the name St Emilion preceded by the name of a village. These wines are of a rich ruby colour. Neighbouring districts include Pomerol, Côtés de Canon Fronsac, Lalande de Pomerol, Neac, Côtés de Fronsac, St Georges, Lussac, Montagne, Parsac and Puisseguin. Between the rivers Garonne and Dordogne is produced the wine of Entre-Deux-Mers, a dry white wine with a subtle bouquet. Above Bordeaux the Médoc vineyards are planted on stony and sandy	71

Navigations	Km	Locks	Towns and Villages	Michelin Map No
RIVER GARONNE			ground on the left bank of the Gironde. According to an old saying the vines must be planted on stony ground and in sight of the river for the wine to be good. Stretching from the Point de Grave to Bordeaux the vineyard is divided into two parts, Médoc in the North and Haut-Médoc in the Southern part. Some of the finest red wines in the world are produced here: Médoc is fine, generally light red. The superior subdistricts belonging to Haut-Médoc are St Estèphe, Pauillac, St Julien, Listrac, Moulis, Margaux. To the right of the Gironde are the seven districts where Cognac is made. The town of Cognac is 60 km (37 M) away. If intending to stay, pass through lock into basin.	

Bordeaux.

Navigations	Km	Locks	Towns and Villages	Michelin Map No
RIVER GARONNE				
From right River Dordogne. From this point the River Garonne becomes the River Gironde	21			
	105		**Royan** (pop: 18 000). Popular seaside resort with several beaches of fine sand. There are a number of interesting examples of modern architecture, as a result of the destruction of the town in World War II. Ferry terminal. Marina.	71

Just above Royan, opposite the northern end of the Ile d'Oleron at Port-des-Barques, you can enter the River Charente. It is not connected to any other waterway but the navigation facilities have been improved over the 160 km (99 M) to Angoulême. There is a marina at Rochefort and a cruiser hire base at Cognac. From the quay here the unmistakably perfumed air leads you to Hennessy or Otard, a reason enough for exploring the Charente.

Route 1A
Branch from Canal du Midi to La Nouvelle

Distance: **37 km (23 M)**   Number of Locks: **13**   Minimum height above water: **3.10 m**
Minimum depth of water: **1.75 m**

Navigations	Km	Locks	Towns and Villages	Michelin Map No
From CANAL DU MIDI			**Mirepeisset** (near)	83
		5		
	3		**Salleles** Quay, village.	83
		2		
RIVER AUDE CANAL DE LA ROBINE	3			
		3		
	8		**Narbonne** (pop: 42 000). Interesting old town, a seaport long ago until silting up occurred. Boulevards now where ramparts used to be. 13th C former Archbishop's palace. Museum. The vineyards of Minervois, a wine-growing area since Roman times, are situated across the two departments of Aude and Hérault, beginning just above Carcassone and ending around Narbonne. The dry and warm climate produces a VDQS wine of excellent quality, mostly red.	83, 86
		3		
	23		**Port la Nouvelle** (pop: 2000). Small commercial and fishing port with resort-type development. We have stepped our mast here in an emergency. Harbour basin and Mediterranean.	86

Route 2
Beaucaire to Sète
Distance: **103 km (648 M)**   Number of Locks: **2**
Minimum height above water (but see Petit Rhône to Grau d'Orgon): **4.75 m**
Minimum depth of water: **1.80 m**
The Canal du Rhône à Sète cannot be reached through the lock opposite Tarascon as
formerly, although access may be restored one day. Entry to it is from the Rhône at
K 265, into the Petit Rhône and through the Ecluse St Gilles at K 29.

Navigations	Km Mk	Locks	Towns and Villages	Michelin Map No
See plan on page 37.	0		**Beaucaire** (pop: 13 000). Its fair, first held in 1217, was famous throughout Western Europe until the 19th C but is of little importance now. Wine shipping port. Ruins of 13th C castle; fine views over Rhône from remaining tower. Museum with local relics and items referring to the fair. Large boat harbour.	
LOCK DU NOURRIGUIER	8	1		
			Saint Gilles Basin. Hire craft.	
Junction with **PETIT RHÔNE**	29			

Petite Rhône to Grau d'Orgon				
RIVER RHONE *Turn* RIGHT *into* **PETIT RHONE** *(Km Mk numbering continues in sequence)*	279			
Junction STRAIGHT ON *to Grau d'Orgon (maximum height 2.70 m)*	299			
Care necessary proceeding to sea	377		**Grau d'Orgon**	

Navigations	Km Mk	Locks	Towns and Villages	Michelin Map No
Petit Rhône to the Canal du Rhône à Sète				
RIVER RHÔNE *turn* RIGHT into **PETIT RHÔNE**	279			
Junction turn RIGHT	299			
LOCK ST GILLES	300	1		
Join **CANAL DU RHONE À SÈTE** (*Km Mk numbering of Canal du Rhône à Sète*)	29 50		**Aigues-Mortes** (pop: 4000). Walled town with 17 towers and 10 gates, in the middle of swamps and lagoons from which its name (*aquae mortuae*, dead waters) derives. Founded by St Louis in the 13th C as a Mediterranean seaport, but much silting up since. Church of St Louis 13 C. The canal has been upgraded to take large barges.	83
LEFT *Canal Maritime to Le Grau du Roi*	75		**Palavas**	
	92		**Frontignan** Basin.	
LEFT *to Sète* Straight on to Bassin du Thau and across to Canal du Midi to join with Routes 1 and 1A.	96		**Sète** (pop: 36 000). Interesting commercial port with many canals lined with boats of all sorts. Busy fishing harbour and separate marina-type yacht harbour. Large export trade in wine.	83

Route 3
Berry-au-Bac to Maxilly-à-Saône

Distance: **315 km (195 M)**   Number of locks: **143**   Minimum height above water: **3.50 m**
Minimum depth of water: **2.13 m**

Navigations	Km	Locks	Towns and Villages	Michelin Map No
CANAL DE L'AISNE A MARNE		6	**Berry-au-Bac** Fuel and many other facilities.	56
	10	3	**Loivre**	56
	13		**Rheims** (pop: 180 000). Splendid modern city, rebuilt after damage of two world wars. Many kings of France were crowned here. Centre of champagne producing region. Germans surrendered in Rheims in May 1945. Notre Dame cathedral, 13th C; St Rémy church, 11th C. Museum: pictures (Delacroix, Latour, Bonnard, Gauguin, Matisse, Picasso, Pissarro, Renoir, Sisley), sculptures, tapestries. The following Champagne Cellars in Rheims can be visited: Veuve-Clicquot-Ponsardin, Pommery et Greno, Taittinger, Piper-Heidsieck, Mumm, Ruinart Pere et Fils, Abel Lepitre, Charles Heidsieck, George Goulet, Heidsieck & Co Monopole, Henriot, Lanson, Louis Roederer, and Masse Pere et Fils. Times and details from *Syndicat d'Initiative*. Most offer free tasting. Moorings not very restful.	56
CANAL LATERAL A LA MARNE		4		
	11	3	**Sillery** Shops nearby. Quay.	56
	10	2	**Sept-Saulx** Pleasant moorings and shops.	56
Tunnel	3	8		
LEFT *continuing* **CANAL LATERAL A LA MARNE**	10	2	**Conde-sur-Marne**	56

Navigations	Km	Locks	Towns and Villages	Michelin Map No
RIGHT *to Epernay, River Marne* CANAL LATERAL A LA MARNE	16		**Châlons-sur-Marne** (pop: 54 000). Capital of the department of Marne. Old town with a busy trade in wine, centre of the champagne country. Many fine buildings and pleasant tree-lined avenues. Suffered damage in both world wars. Variety of industry including Perrier. Cathedral, St Etienne, 13th C. Churches: Notre-Dame en Vaux, 12th C; St Loup, 15th C; St Jean Baptiste, 11th–14th C. Museum: prehistoric, Gallo-Roman, Merovingian discoveries, sculptures, pictures. Moorings, barges and shops.	
	11	3	**St Germain-la-Ville** Some shops.	56, 61
	10	1	**Ablancourt**	61
LEFT *Canal de la Marne au Rhin* STRAIGHT ON **CANAL DE LA MARNE A LA SAONE**	11	5	**Vitry-le-François** (pop: 15 000). Once fortified town. Badly war damaged in 1940 and since rebuilt. All facilities.	61
	19	8	**Perthes** Quay.	61
	11	6	**St Dizier** (pop: 35 000). Industrial town, rebuilt after disastrous 18th C fire. Part of old castle remains. St Martin church, 13th C. Moorings, yacht harbour. Good facilities.	61, 62
	6	2	**Chamouilley** Quay.	61, 62
	8	4	**Bayard-sur-Marne** Quay	61, 62
	16	7	**Joinville.** Small old town. 16th C château. Quay.	61, 62
	13	6	**Gudmont** Quay.	61, 62
		4		

Navigations	Km	Locks	Towns and Villages	Michelin Map No
CANAL DE LA MARNE A LA SAONE	13		**Vouecourt.** From here (or from Bologne eight km (5 M) further on) it is about 13 km (8 km (8 M) to Colombey-les-deux-Eglises, Quay.	
		4		
	8		**Bologne** Moorings.	61, 62
		5		
Tunnel	8			
		1		
	3		**Chaumont** (pop: 29 000). Pleasantly situated town. Fine buildings. Centre for manufacture of gloves and leather work. Headquarters of the American Army in World War I. Church: St John, 13th C. Castle, 10th C. Quay.	61, 62
		8		
CANAL DE LA MARNE A LA SAONE	13		**Foulain** Pleasant moorings and shops.	62
	13	7	**Rolampoint** Convenient moorings and shops.	66
		5		
	6		**Humes** Quay.	66
		3		
	5		**Langres** (pop: 11 500). Old walled town in beautiful setting. St Mammes Cathedral, 12th C. Two museums: sculptures, natural history, enamels, ivories, book-bindings. Basin.	66
		1		
	6		**Balesmes-sur-Marne**	66
Tunnel				
	2		**Heuilley-Cotton** Basin.	66
		5		
	8		**Villegusien** Convenient shops. Basin.	66
		13		
	13		**Cusey** Basin.	66
		5		
	11		**La Villeneuve-sur-Vingeanne** Quay.	66
		10		
	18		**Oisilly** Quay.	66
		3		
Junction with River Saone	11		**Maxilly-à-Saône** Quay.	66

Route 4
Berry-au-Bac to Troussey

Distance: **268 km (166 M)**   Number of Locks: **93**   Minimum height above water: **3.35 m**
Minimum depth of water: **1.98 m**

Navigations	Km	Locks	Towns and Villages	Michelin Map No
CANAL LATERAL A L'AISNE			Berry-au-Bac Basin.	56
		1		
	5	1	Variscourt Quay.	56
	2		Pignicourt Quay.	56
	2		Neufchatel-sur-Aisne	56
CANAL DES ARDENNES	5		Vieux-les-Asfeld Pleasant village with various shops. Quay.	56
		2		
	5		Asfeld Quay.	56
		2		
	11		Château-Porcien	56
	5		Nanteuil-sur-Aisne Quay.	56
		2		
	3		Rethel (pop: 9000). Much damaged in both world wars and rebuilt twice. Church: St Nicholas, 13th C. Folklore museum. Best shopping facilities. Quay.	56
		3		
	11		Ambly Quay.	56
		1		
	5		Givry Quay.	56
		1		
	3		Attigny Quay.	56
		3		
	6		Semuy	56
		6		
	3		Neuville Quay.	56
		8		

Navigations	Km	Locks	Towns and Villages	Michelin Map No
CANAL DES ARDENNES	3		**Montgon**	56
		11		
	3		**Le Chesne** Mooring convenient for shops.	56
		2		
	13		**Ambly**	56
		1		
	3		**Malmy** Quay.	56
	3		**Omicourt** 2 kms (1¼ M) ahead is the St Aignan tunnel. Quay.	53
Tunnel		2		
	6		**Hannogne-St Martin** Pleasant village with shops.	53
		2		
RIGHT *into* **CANAL DE L'EST.**	2		Pont-a-Bar	53
		1		
LEFT *to River Meuse and Belgian frontier.*	3		**Donchery**	53
		1		
	8		**Sedan** (pop: 25 000). Busy industrial town. Much damaged in World War II, but now rebuilt. Quay.	53
		1		
	6		**Remilly** Quay.	53, 56
		1		
	6		**Mouzon** Quay.	56
		2		
	10		**Inor** Quay, village.	56
		2		
	8		**Stenay** Quays. Small town.	56
		2		
	13		**Dun-sur-Meuse** Shops nearby. Quay. Charter craft base.	56
		5		
	18		**Consevoye** Village.	56
		4		
	15		**Bras-sur Meuse** Village.	57
	8		**Verdun-sur-Meuse** Convenient moorings in town.	57

Le Chesne.

Navigations	Km	Locks	Towns and Villages	Michelin Map No
CANAL DE L'EST				
Tunnel	14	5	**Dieue** Supermarket nearby. Quay.	57
	3		**Genicourt-sur-Meuse** Quay. Village.	57
	3		**Ambly-sur-Meuse** Basin nearby.	57
		2		
	5		**Troyon** Quay.	57
		1		
	3		**Lacroix-sur-Meuse.** Basin. Village nearby.	57
		1		
	11		**St Mihiel** Moorings and shops.	57
		3		

St Aignan tunnel.

Navigations	Km	Locks	Towns and Villages	Michelin Map No
CANAL DE L'EST	11		**Sampigny** Quay. Village.	57
		2		
	11		**Commercy** (pop: 9000). Pleasantly situated small town. Shops near quay.	62
		1		
	8		**Vertuzey**	62
		4		
RIGHT *Canal de la Marne au Rhin*	5		**Troussey**	62

Route 5
Calais to Watten
Distance: **30 km (18 M)**   Number of Locks: **1**   Minimum height above water: **3.55 m**
Minimum depth of water: **2.28 m**

Navigations	Km	Locks	Towns and Villages	Michelin Map No
CANAL DE CALAIS			**Calais** (pop: 77 000). Busy cross-Channel port and seaside resort with miles of fine sand. Much damaged during World War II, rebuilt on modern lines. English base during World War I. Nearest French town to England. Calais and Dover were first	51

The Port de Plaisance, Calais.

Le Port de Plaisance de Calais.

Navigations	Km	Locks	Towns and Villages	Michelin Map No
CANAL DE CALAIS			linked by a regular packet service over 200 years ago; Calais now receives 1 500 000 British travellers a year. Leading industry: machine lace and tulle. Museum: Flemish linen and lace, Rodin's 'Burghers of Calais'. War museum. Monuments. Enter the Bassin Ouest, ($1\frac{1}{2}$ hours before HW to $\frac{1}{2}$ hour after), to the yacht club, visitors pontoon to S. Good club facilities, mast lowering etc.	
RIGHT *into Canal de Guines*	8		**Les Attaques** Quay. Automatic lifting bridge.	
RIGHT *into Canal d'Ardres*	3			
RIGHT *into Canal d'Audruicq*	10		**Fort Batard** Quay.	
		1	**Hennuin** New lock, automatically linked to lifting bridge.	
Turn RIGHT *into* **RIVER AA**	14		**Watten** Quay.	51

Route 5A
Dunkirk to Watten

Distance: **32 km (20 M)**   Number of locks: **2**   Minimum height above water: **3.50 m**
Minimum depth of water: **2.13 m**

Navigations	Km	Locks	Towns and Villages	Michelin Map No
DUNKERQUE-ESCAUT WATERWAY		1	**Dunkirk** (pop: 73 000). Famous for the evacuation of the British Expeditionary Force in 1940 during which the town was almost completely destroyed; now rebuilt on modern lines. One of the most important seaports in France with big refineries and steelworks; connected to the inland industrial regions by four canals. Birthplace of Jean Bart, famous 17th C sailor.	51
Turn right into **CANAL DE BOURBOURG**		1		
	24		**Watten** Quay.	51

Dunkerque showing Port de Plaisance, centre and municipal marina lower right.

Route 6
Chalon-sur-Saône to Lyon

Distance: **139 km (86 M)**   Number of locks: **5**   Minimum height above water: **3.45 m**
Minimum depth of water: **1.98 m**

Navigations	Km	Locks	Towns and Villages	Michelin Map No
RIVER SAONE			**Chalon-sur-Saône** Harbour.	70
		1		
	31		**Tournus** (pop: 7000). Moorings on the quay by the bridge.	70
	10		**Uchizy** Nearby wine village of Chardonnay.	70
	5		**Port Fleurville** Moorings and nearby shops.	70
By-pass Canal	16		**Mâcon** (pop: 26 000). Busy commercial town in the centre of wine-growing country, the Mâconnais. Old walled gardens and vineyards. Birthplace of Lamartine. Cathedral remains, 13th C, used as archaeological museum. The Mâconnais white grapes (Pinot, Chardonnay) give Mâcon Blanc and the Pouillys (especially Pouilly-Fuisse) the characteristic nutty flavour. The black Gamay grape produces the sprightly Mâcon Rouge and Mâcon Rosé. Nearby wine villages of Solutré, Pouilly, Fousse. Along the Saône are the Beaujolais villages, producing a soft, fruity wine, best drunk young and fresh. On the granite slopes west and northwards are the great vineyards of St Amour, Julienas, Chenas, Moulin-à-Vent, Fleurie, Chiroubles, Morgon, and Brouilly, delicate, light, lively wines with a rich bouquet. Moorings, fuel, water and all services available at Port de Plaisance.	70

Chalon-sur-Saône.
Opposite the 'barge parking' turn in, towards the distant bridge . . .

. . . under which is the Port de Plaisance, with toilets, showers etc.

Navigations	Km	Locks	Towns and Villages	Michelin Map No
RIVER SAONE	6		**Creches** Nearby wine villages of St Amour (tasting at Caveau St Armour), Julienas.	73
	8		**St Roman-des-Iles** Nearby wine villages of Chenas, le Moulin-à-Vent (tasting at Caveau au Pied du Moulin), Fleurie. Fuel available. Harbour.	73
	3	1	**Thoissey** (pop: 1000). Nearby wine villages of Chiroubles, Morgon.	73
	10		**Belleville-sur-Saône** Nearby wine village of Brouilly. Quay.	73
	3		**Montmerle-sur-Saône** Quay.	73

Lyon.

Navigations	Km	Locks	Towns and Villages	Michelin Map No
RIVER SAONE	11		**Villefranche-sur Saône** (pop: 29 000). Important industrial town and wine centre. Interesting old house. Notre-Dame church, 12th C.	73
	10		**Trevoux** Moorings by disused bridge. Boatyard.	73
		1		
	10		**Neuville-sur-Saône** Moorings and shops.	73
		2		
	16		**Lyon** (pop: 550 000). Third largest city in France. Centre of textile industry, particularly silk weaving, but much other industry besides. The most important buildings and shops are in the area between the Rhône and the Saône and adjacent to the yacht mooring. The hill of Fourvière with the modern church of Notre-Dame at its summit may be ascended by funicular railway. Churches: St Martin, 11th C; St Nizier, 15th C. Museum: old furniture, tapestries, watercolours, coins. Collection of oriental carpets. Also Delacroix, Gauguin, Manet, Renoir.	73
Confluence with River Rhône				

Route 7
Chauny to Berry-au-Bac

Distance: **72 km (44 M)**   Number of Locks: **14**   Minimum height above water: **3.37m**
Minimum depth of water: **2.21 m**

Navigations	Km	Locks	Towns and Villages	Michelin Map No
CANAL LATERAL A L'OISE			**Chauny** Quays.	56
LEFT *into* CANAL DE L'OISE A L'AISNE RIGHT *to* Compiègne	2	1	**Abbecourt** Quay.	56
	5		**Champs** Quay. Village.	56
	3	4	**Guny** Quay. Village.	56
	15	4	**Anizy** Good shops. Basin.	56
Tunnel	11		**Pargny-Filain** Basin.	56
	6	4	**Braye-en-Laonnois** Village.	56
	6		**Bourg-et-Comin** Quay. Village.	56
LEFT *into* CANAL LATERAL A L'AISNE	4	1		
RIGHT *to Soissons*	20		**Berry-au-Bac** Basin. Village nearby.	56

Route 8
Chauny to Conflans St Honorine

Distance: **141 km (87 M)**   Number of locks: **11**   Minimum height above water: **4.04 m**
Minimum depth of water: **2.44 m**

Navigations	Km	Locks	Towns and Villages	Michelin Map No
CANAL LATERAL A L'OISE			**Chauny** Fuel available. Quay. Town centre.	56
LEFT *Canal de l'Oise à l'Aisne*				
	3		**Abbecourt** Basin. Boatyard.	56
	5		**Appilly** Quay. Village.	56
		2		
	16		**Pimprez** Village.	56
	2		**Ribecourt** Nearby shops. Quay.	56
		1		
	6		**Montmacq**	56
		1		
	3		**Longueil** Village.	56
RIVER OISE				
	2		**Janville** Village.	56
LEFT *into River Aisne*	3			
	2		**Compiègne** (pop: 43 000). A popular place for tourists attracted by the great palace and enormous forest (33 000 acres, one of the largest in France), for long a favourite hunting resort of the kings of France. Joan of Arc was captured here on 23 May 1430 by John of Luxembourg who handed her over to the English. The palace is now a museum; the rooms occupied by Marie Antoinette, Napoléon I and III can be seen; also the National Automobile Museum with 150 vehicles ranging from the Roman chariot to the Citroën chaintrack car. Nearby in the forest is the clearing in which Marshal Foch received	56

Navigations	Km	Locks	Towns and Villages	Michelin Map No
RIVER OISE			the German surrender in November 1918; and where Hitler received the French surrender in 1940. The original railway saloon car was destroyed in World War II, but a replica may be seen. Town Hall Museum: historical miniature figures, the only French museum of lead soldiers (90 000), with a large scene of the Battle of Waterloo. Quayside moorings and Port de Plaisance.	
		1		
	6		**Jaux** Quay. Charter craft.	56
		1		
	10		**Verberie** Moorings and shops.	56
		1		
	11		**Pont St Maxence** Industrial, but moorings available.	56
	12		**Creil** (pop: 20 000). Industrial town. Church: St Médard, 12th C. Quays.	56
		1		
	6		**St Leu-d'Esserent** Moorings and shops.	56
	6		**Precy-sur-Oise** Moorings and shops.	56
	3		**Boran-sur-Oise** A pleasure craft	56
		1	atmosphere with quay, shops and restaurants.	
	10		**Beaumont-sur-Oise** Commercial quays.	55
		1		
	7		**L'Isle-Adam** Small town.	55
	13		**Pontoise** (pop:19 000). Interesting old town with hilly, narrow streets. Churches: St Maclou, 12th C; Notre-Dame, 13th C. Quay, moorings, shops and other facilities.	55
		1		
	13		**Conflans St Honorine** Home of the barge trade. All facilities here if you can get alongside.	55

Route 9
Compiègne to Bourg-et-Comin

Distance: **65 km (40 M)**   Number of Locks: **10**   Minimum height above water: **3.35 m**
Minimum depth of water: **2.05 m**

Navigations	Km	Locks	Towns and Villages	Michelin Map No
RIVER OISE			**Compiègne** (See page 118)	56
RIGHT *into* **RIVER**		3		
AISNE	18		**Attichy** Quay. Village.	56
		1		
	6		**Vic-sur-Aisne** Interesting village with shops. Quay.	56
		2		
	18		**Soissons** (pop: 32 000). Industrial town, much damaged in both world wars and since rebuilt. Cathedral: St Gervais, 12th C. Busy quay but good shopping.	56
		1		
	11		**Missy** Quay. Village.	56
RIGHT *to* **CANAL**	5		**Conde-sur-Aisne** Quay.	56
LATERAL A				
L'AISNE		3		
LEFT *to* **CANAL DE**				
L'OISE A L'AISNE	7		**Bourg-et-Comin** Some shops. Quay.	56

Route 10
Laroche to Decize

Distance: **192 km (119 M)** Number of locks: **110** Minimum height above water: **2.67 m**
Minimum depth of water: **1.57 m**

Navigations	Km	Locks	Towns and Villages	Michelin Map No
RIVER YONNE			**Laroche** Quay. Village.	65
LEFT *Canal de Bourgogne*		2		
	6		**Bassou** Village.	65
		7		
	16		**Auxerre** (pop: 42 000). Capital of the department of Yonne. Centre of wine and beautiful district of vineyards and orchards. An old town built on a hill, a	65
CANAL DU NIVERNAIS			most attractive sight from the river. St Germain's Abbey, Caroligian crypts, 9th C frescoes (the oldest mural paintings in France), 12th C Romanesque spire. St Etienne, 13th C. Museums with Napoleonic souvenirs, early French paintings, tapestries. Quay, moorings and Port de Plaisance. Fuel and all facilities.	
		8		

Auxerre.

Briare. Canal latéral à la Loire. Pont canal, 640 m (699 yds) long, built by Eiffel in 1890 to carry the Briare Canal over the River Loire.

Navigations	Km	Locks	Towns and Villages	Michelin Map No
LEFT *Canal de Bourgogne*	13		**Vincelles** Fuel and shops. Quay.	65
		9		
	18		**Mailly-le-Château** Convenient shops.	65
		9		
	19		**Coulanges-sur-Yonne** Fuel and shops. Quay.	65
		4		
	10		**Clamecy** (pop: 6000). The old city of the Counts of Nevers, situated at the confluence of the Yonne and the Beuvron, a cultural centre, the birthplace of Romain Rolland and Claude Tillier. Moorings, shops and all facilities. Charter craft.	65
		6		
	10		**Breves** Basin. Village.	65
		5		
	11		**Dirol** Quay.	65
		6		
	10		**Chaumot** Quay. Charter craft.	65
		11		
	9		**Sardy-les-Epiry** Basin. Village.	65
		16		
	5			
Tunnel	2		**Baye** Quay. Charter craft.	69
		8		
	15		**Chatillon-en-Bazois** A small town of character. Moorings.	68
		12		
	22		**Pannecot** Moorings. Village.	69
		5		
	13		**Cercy-la-Tour** Pleasant town with good shops. Quay.	69
		2		
LEFT *to* **CANAL LATERAL A LA LOIRE**	13		**Decize** (pop: 7500). An old town with a church built on a 7th C crypt. Promenade des Halles leads to the beach and water sports stadium. Convenient moorings and all shops.	69

Route 11
Le Havre to Paris

Distance: **364 km (226 M)**   Number of locks: **7**   Minimum height above water: **5.97 m**
Minimum depth of water: **3.18 m**

Because Le Havre is the most popular entry port into France, the alternatives here will be dealt with at some length.

On arrival at Le Havre, a yacht should turn hard to port immediately on passing through the harbour entrance and proceed to the appropriate yacht moorings ahead in the Ports des Yachts. Sailing yachts can have their masts unstepped here by a small crane on the jetty.

From Le Havre it is possible in a yacht of only moderate speed to reach Rouen (128 km) (79 M) on one tide going straight up the Seine. From the Petit Port, returning out of the harbour entrance and across to the entrance of the Seine will take approximately an hour. It is advisable to have Admiralty Chart 2990. Obviously it is essential to be ready, moving up the Seine just before the first of the flood. In good weather this is the easiest, quickest, and most agreeable way of reaching Rouen.

(An alternative to Le Havre, about 20 km (12 M) away up the

Petit Port, Le Havre.

Seine, is Honfleur, but it is necessary to lock in and out here with the inevitable wait for the tide. The locks open for about an hour either side of high water.)

On several tides each side of springs and particularly at equinoctial springs, the tidal bore phenomenon known as the Mascaret occurs in the lower Seine almost to Rouen. Reaching its greatest magnitude at Caudebec, a wave height of 6 m can occur there if there is a westerly wind. Victor Hugo lost his eldest daughter and her husband in the Mascaret of 4 September 1843; they were drowned in front of his house at Villequier. Since then the power of the Mascaret has been much lessened by·various river works, but it is still a consideration to be taken into account when planning the time-table of a voyage up the Seine.

Having reached the Petit Port, if the weather outside is bad it is not necessary to leave the protection of Le Havre harbour. An alternative route is to proceed through Le Havre docks and up the Tancarville Canal (24 km (15 M), 2 locks), a slower and less pleasant waterway. To reach the Tancarville Canal from the Petit Port the correct route is via the Avant Port, Arrière Port, Bassin de la Citadelle, Bassin de l'Eure, Bassin Fluvial (*not* the

Bassin du Commerce, Le Havre.

Basin Bellot which is for big ships only),Bassin Vétillart, and so
to the Canal de Tancarville.

On arrival at Tancarville lock it will almost certainly be
necessary to wait for locking in. Secure out of the way of
commercial traffic, between the mooring posts and the bank, for
instance, rather than on the 'channel' side of the posts. The
Tancarville lock opening schedule is linked to the times of the
Seine tides; you will only be let out into the Seine at the right
time.

On coming out of the Tancarville lock, a good look-out must
be kept for traffic coming down the Seine as it will obviously be
necessary to cross the path of this traffic to get to the correct
side of the river.

Craft with sufficient power usually proceed straight up the
Seine to Rouen without stopping at Le Havre.

Navigations	Km	Locks	Towns and Villages	Michelin Map No
RIVER SEINE			**Le Havre** (pop: 200 000). The second largest seaport in France and principal transatlantic port in the country. It suffered greater damage in World War II than any other port. Rebuilding of the town was carefully planned with wide streets; the first of these seen on coming from the yacht harbour at the Petit Port is the Avenue Foch leading to the Town Hall Square.	55
			Honfleur (pop: 9000). Picturesque houses round the old harbour are an attractive feature of this charming old town. The church of St Catherine was built of wood by local shipbuilders. Fishing boats and yachts use the harbour; despite need to lock in and out, many yachtsmen prefer it to Le Havre.	55
LEFT *into Tancarville Canal*	21		**Tancarville** Tancarville Bridge, the longest suspension bridge in Europe, was completed in 1959.	55

Navigations	Km	Locks	Towns and Villages	Michelin Map No
RIVER SEINE	29		**Caudebec-en-Caux** Picturesque little timber-built town, largely destroyed in World War II. Popular place to view the Mascaret.	55
	65		**Rouen** Yacht harbour. Pré au Loup. Important industrial town, although inland is the third largest seaport in France with 24 km (15 M) of docks and wharves. Much damaged in World War II and rebuilt on modern lines. Joan of Arc was burned alive in Rouen in 1431; the site on the Place du Vieux-Marche is marked and there is a statue nearby of Joan at the stake. Cathedral: Notre-Dame, 13th C. Museum: fine arts, one of the best in France, Corot, Delacroix, Fragonard, Ingrès, Monet, Renoir, Sisley. Bassin St Gervais is the usual berth if stopping for the night, but it is not very near to town. A sailing yacht cannot proceed beyond Rouen without unstepping the mast.	55

Rouen.

Navigations	Km	Locks	Towns and Villages	Michelin Map No
RIVER SEINE	24		**Elbeuf** (pop: 19 000). Industrial town, centre of cloth making industry.	55
		1		
	45		**Les Andelys** (pop: 8000). Pretty little place in beautiful situation, by the Forest of Andelys. Château Gaillard ruins, built by Richard the Lionheart in 1196. Yacht harbour.	55
		1		
	24		**Vernon** (pop: 23 000). Pleasant town. Notre-Dame Church, 12th C. Tour Guise erected by King Henry I of England.	56
		1		
	10		**Bonniéres** Commercial quay.	55
		1		
	28		**Mantes** (pop: 15 000). Old town in pretty situation. Much damaged in World War II but 12th C Notre-Dame church survived.	55

Château Gaillard, Les Andelys.

Navigations	Km	Locks	Towns and Villages	Michelin Map No
			William the Conqueror fatally injured here in falling from his horse. Port de Plaisance de l'Ilon.	
	28		**Poissy** Yacht harbour.	55
LEFT *River Oise*		1		
	11		**Conflans St Honorine** Home base of the barge trade. Note the barge painted white and bearing a cross; this is the floating chapel of the *bateliers*.	55
		2		
	23		**Bougival** Triple lock.	55
	50		**Paris** (pop: 3 000 000). The Touring Club de France 3-deck Headquarters boat is on the port side immediately past Pont Alexandre III but their moorings extend from Point Invalides to Pont de la Concorde. There are other moorings in	55

Touring Club de France, Paris.

Navigations	Km	Locks	Towns and Villages	Michelin Map No
RIVER SEINE			Paris, but this is most central, provides the best facilities and information. A few steps from the TCF mooring is the Place de la Concorde and the Tuileries Gardens. Also on the same side of the river, The Louvre, Palais Royal, Comédie Française, Avenue de l'Opéra, Opéra House, the Grand Boulevards, Madeleine Church, rue Royale, rue de la Paix, Place Vendôme, rue de Rivoli, Faubourg Saint-Honoré, Avenue des Champs-Elysées connecting the Place de la Concorde with the Place de l'Etoile, and the Arc de Triomphe.	

A great deal of river traffic passes.

Navigations	Km	Locks	Towns and Villages	Michelin Map No

RIVER SEINE

On the other side of the river, the Palais Bourbon (National Assembly), Quai d'Orsay (Foreign Office), Esplanade des Invalides, the Hôtel des Invalides with the tombs of Napoléon and Marshal Foch, the Eiffel Tower. Worth a visit is the Musée des Caves de la Tour Eiffel, under the Chaillot Hill, Square Charles Dickens, Paris 16; with mile-long galleries, wine museum, history of wine, a guided tour, and wine tasting.

The Touring Club Headquarters offers hot showers, bar and restaurant facilities,

Bateau Mouche. *Photo Lucien Viguier*

Navigations	Km	Locks	Towns and Villages	Michelin Map No
RIVER SEINE				

fuel and water. They are very helpful with any tourist query, but particularly with up-to-date news of the state of the waterways. English speaking staff are available much of the time.

However, during the day there is a great deal of river traffic past the TCF moorings – barge, Coche d'Eau, Bateau Mouche, and Vedette Tour Eiffel – setting up a continuous swell and the Port de Plaisance de Paris – Arsenal is preferred.

Port de Plaisance de Paris-Arsenal From the Touring Club de France, mentioned on page 129, past the Ile de la Cite and the Ile St Louis, after the Pont de Sully and just

Paris-Arsenal, with kind permission of Apese Cartographie.

Navigations	Km	Locks	Towns and Villages	Michelin Map No

RIVER SEINE

before the Pont d'Auterlitz, you turn left in through a small lock. There is a holding pontoon where you can secure while you talk to the *Capitainerie* (English is understood) over the intercom. You will already have been observed on their screen. When the traffic lights change in your favour, locking in is easy and you tie up by the *Capitainerie* to be given your berth number. Locking in is automatic, operated remotely from the Harbour Master's office.

There are 177 berths, with 65 reserved for overnight stops. Berths are available on a yearly, monthly or daily basis. It can accommodate craft of from 6 to 25 metres

With kind permission of Apese Cartographie.

Navigations	Km	Locks	Towns and Villages	Michelin Map No
			and water and power are included. There is a restaurant overlooking the Dock and a garden and children's play area.	

Draft at harbour entrance: 1.9 m
VHF radio: Channel 19
Opening hours: April–October
    Lock 0800–2345
    Harbour office 0900–1800 (open until
    2000 at week-ends in summer)
Facilities: washrooms, launderette, telephone, oil discharge, crane (7 tonnes), petrol, car park, restaurant, with a security fence all round.

Specimen charges (French francs)

LOA	Day (April–September)	Month	Year
10 metre	122	2.670	19.300
12 metre	154	3.560	27.000
16 metre	198	4.160	36.800

Enquiries should be made to: Capitainerie du Port de Plaisance de Paris-Arsenal, Pleasure Harbour, 11 Boulevard de la Bastille, 75012. Telephone: 33(1) 43 41 39 32.

The canals of Paris

The canals of Paris, the Canal de l'Ourcq, Canal Saint-Denis and the Canal Saint Martin, have not often been explored because they have been dominated by commercial traffic. The Canal Saint-Denis runs through an industrial area lined with wharves, but there are shops beyond. You enter the Canal Saint Martin when you go into the Paris-Arsenal harbour from the Seine and you need to persevere through and beyond the eerie tunnels to discover the rest of it. Then there is more to explore on the Canal de l'Ourcq.

Coming upstream, you could enter the Canal Saint-Denis from the Seine opposite the Ile Saint-Denis; although the area generally is dominated by warehouses, some awaiting demolition, the exception is the magnificent Saint-Denis Cathedral, situated by the Saint-Denis Basilique metro station. There are seven locks in its length of 6 km (3.7 M) and it leads into the Canal de l'Ourcq and the Canal Saint Martin and the Paris-Arsenal Marina.

Entering the Canal Saint-Denis from the Seine, at the end of this canal you turn right towards the Canal Saint Martin, the Port de Plaisance de Paris-Arsenal and the Seine beyond, or left to the Canal de l'Ourcq which is made up of three sections. From the junction with the Canal Saint-Denis, under the Boulevard Peripherique, the 11 km (7 M) to the Pavillons-sur-Bois is the widened section, from there the 85 km (53 M) to Mareuil is the narrower section suitable only for quite small cruisers, and from there the canalized River Ourcq runs 12 km (7.5 M) to the Port-au-Perches.

Since the Paris-Arsenal harbour is located at the outlet from the Saint-Martin Canal, it has made yachtsmen more aware of the Paris canals.

The Arsenal Dock was built on the site of the moats of the

Bastille, part of a system of docks and canals built under
Napoleon 1. Situated between the Bastille and the Seine it is
near the historical heart of Paris.

Between the Paris-Arsenal Harbour and the Canal Saint-Denis
junction is the Bassin de la Villette. This part of Paris was once
the densely populated working class area, the main meat market
and abattoirs and related industries spread around the
waterways. Now la Villette is an area of high tech culture, with
the disused abattoirs converted into the Science, Industry and
Technology Museum which is certainly worth seeing; in fact,
the visiting yachtsman should make a point of exploring the
whole Villette complex.

Yachtsmen entering the Port de Plaisance de Paris-Arsenal at
the more usual and convenient entry do so at the Canal Saint-
Martin entrance. Beyond the marina is the entry to the tunnels
by the Bastille, emerging attractively with plane trees lining
cobbled quays, behind them old buildings of Paris resembling
some theatrical backdrop. Beyond is La Villette, some industry
and scenes, both colourful and decaying in turn, with cottages
and painted shacks, factories and empty shells. The Canal de
l'Ourcq follows on.

Navigations	Km	Locks	Towns and Villages	Michelin Map No
CANAL DE L'OURCQ *Junction with Canal Saint-Denis*	3		**Pantin** Basin, shops, metro restaurants.	
		1		
	11		**Sevran** Paris suburb. Lock instructions issued here. Shops, restaurants.	
	13		**Claye-Souilly** Countryside area. Basin, shops.	
	6		**Fresnes-sur-Marne** Lock and village.	
		1		
	7		**Trilbardou** Restaurants and shops, attractive village. River Marne lies below.	
		2		

Navigations	Km	Locks	Towns and Villages	Michelin Map No
CANAL DE L'OURCQ	11		**Gregy-les-Meaux** Old village with all facilities.	
		2		
	16		**Vareddes** Pleasant wooded area. Basin, village, shops, restaurants.	
	4		**Congis-sur-Herouanne** Basin, shops, restaurants, Marne nearby.	
	6		**Lizy-sur-Ourcq** Attractive little town. Basin, shops, railway station.	
	13		**Crouy-sur-Ourcq** Basin, village, railway.	
	3		**Neufchelles** Basin, shops, restaurants.	
	4		**Mareuil-sur-Ourcq** Village, basin, shops, railway, restaurants.	
		3		
CANALIZED RIVER OURCQ	6		**Marolles** Village.	
	2		**La Ferte-Milon** Small town of historical interest. All facilities. Basin.	
		1		
	4		**Port-au-Perches** A small village, pleasant country. End of navigation.	

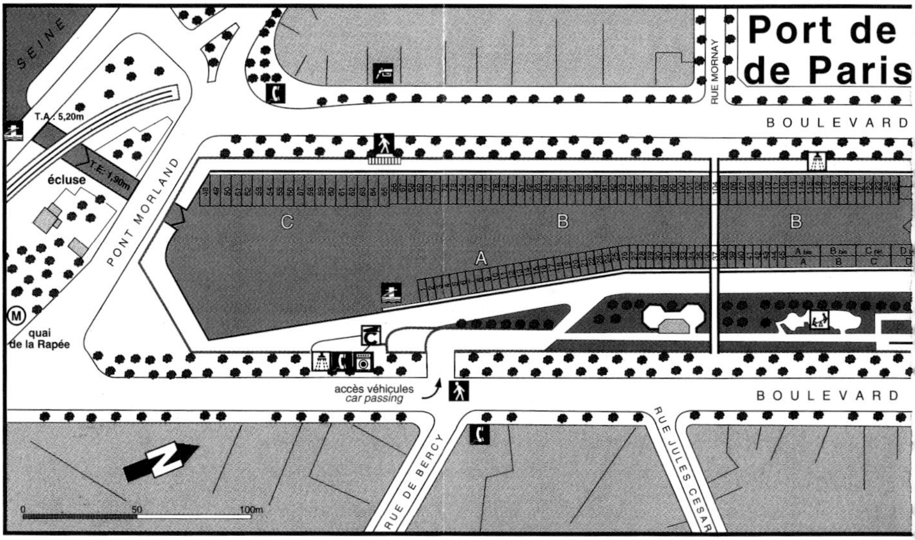
Port de
de Paris
SEINE
T.A.: 5,20m
T.E.: 1,90m
écluse
PONT MORLAND
quai
de la Rapée
RUE MORNAY
BOULEVARD
C
B
B
A
accès véhicules
car passing
BOULEVARD
RUE DE BERCY
RUE JULES CESAR
N
0
50
100m

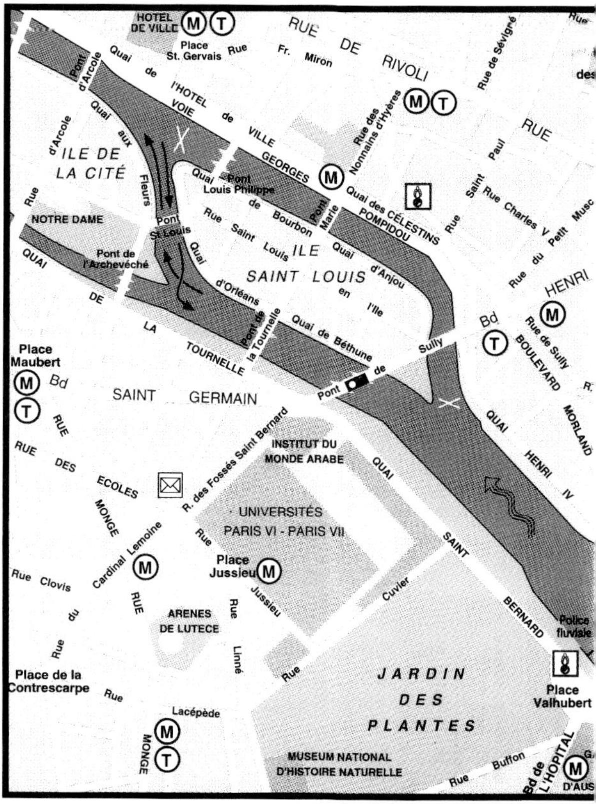
HOTEL DE VILLE
Place St. Gervais
RUE DE RIVOLI
Rue Fr. Miron
Quai de l'HOTEL de VILLE
VOIE GEORGES POMPIDOU
Pont d'Arcole
Quai d'Arcole
Quai aux Fleurs
ILE DE LA CITÉ
NOTRE DAME
Pont de l'Archevéché
Pont St Louis
Pont Louis Philippe
Quai de Bourbon
Rue Saint Louis en l'Ile
ILE SAINT LOUIS
Quai d'Anjou
Quai d'Orléans
Quai de Béthune
Pont Marie
Pont de la Tournelle
Pont de Sully
Quai des CÉLESTINS
Rue des Nonnains d'Hyères
Rue de Sévigné
Rue Saint Paul
Rue Charles V
Rue du Petit Musc
Bd HENRI IV
Rue de Sully
BOULEVARD MORLAND
QUAI HENRI IV
QUAI DE LA TOURNELLE
Place Maubert
Bd SAINT GERMAIN
RUE DES ECOLES
RUE MONGE
R. des Fossés Saint Bernard
INSTITUT DU MONDE ARABE
QUAI SAINT BERNARD
UNIVERSITÉS PARIS VI - PARIS VII
Rue Cardinal Lemoine
Place Jussieu
Rue Jussieu
Rue Clovis
Rue du
ARENES DE LUTECE
Rue Linné
Rue Cuvier
Place de la Contrescarpe
Rue Lacépède
MONGE
JARDIN DES PLANTES
MUSEUM NATIONAL D'HISTOIRE NATURELLE
Rue Buffon
Police fluviale
Place Valhubert
Bd de L'HOPITAL

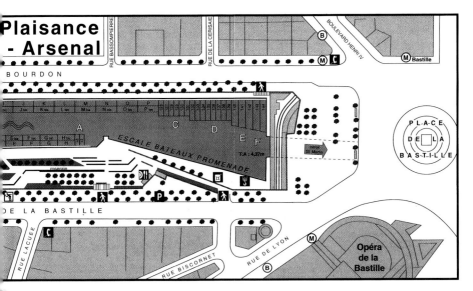

Plan of Port de Plaisance de Paris.

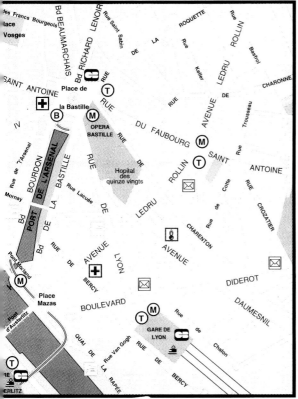

Plan showing entry to Port de L'Arsenal from the Seine.

Route 12
Lyon to Arles

Distance: **308 km (191 M)**   Number of locks: **12**

All Rhône locks are controlled by traffic lights; buzzers acquaint you with the lock operation, that is the raising and lowering of the safety barriers in the front of the upper gates and the opening and closing of the gates/shutters and the movement of the water. Floating bollards, set in the lock walls, carry your warps up or down with you so that no adjustment is necessary.

When going down proceed with care out and under the lifting gates/shutters and look out for considerable quantities of debris collected there.

If you propose 'turning left' when you reach the Mediterranean you will approach it from the Rhône through St Port Louis, the Arles-Fos Canal being closed. If you propose 'turning right' when you reach the Mediterranean you will turn into the Petit Rhône just before Arles and by Km Mark 279, proceeding either to the sea at Grau d'Orgon or through the locks at St Gilles to join the Canal du Rhône à Sète. Locks open between 0500 and 2100 hours.

Navigations	Km Mk	Locks	Towns and Villages	Michelin Map No
RIVER SAONE			Lyon (See page 116)	73
PIERRE-BENITE LOCK	4	1		
RIVER RHONE	24		Vienne (pop: 28 000). Ancient town important in Roman times, but also developed industrially, particularly textiles. Roman Temple of Augustus and Livia, 25 BC Roman Theatre and many other Roman remains. The Côtes-du-Rhône vineyards stretch right along the River Rhône. There are two wine-growing regions, and these are separated from each other by a zone of approximately 64 km (40 M) where there are no vineyards. In the	73

Navigations	Km Mk	Locks	Towns and Villages	Michelin Map No
RIVER RHONE			northern region, which stretches from Vienne down to Valence, the land rises steeply from the river valley and the vines grow on the terraced hillsides. Almost opposite Vienne, on the other bank of the river, one of the most famous and oldest of all the Côtes-du-Rhône red wines is produced, the Côte Rôtie, which has been appreciated since Roman times for its richness. Moorings on quay.	
LOCK DE VAUGRIS		1		
	39		**Les Roches-de-Condrieu** Yacht harbour.	
	41		**Condreiu** Here is produced the distinctive Condrieu, also the rare Château Grillet. For wine-testing, enquiries should be made at the Pavilion de Tourisme. Moorings and shops.	73

Arles.

Navigations	Km Mk	Locks	Towns and Villages	Michelin Map No
LOCK SABLONS	61 70	1	Yacht harbour	
LOCK ST VALLIER-DE-GERVANS	86	1		
	91		**Tournon** (pop: 6500). Busy old town. Near here, on the West bank, are produced the full-flavoured red and white St Joseph wines, the red Cornas, and the sparkling white St Peray. On the opposite bank are the districts of Crozes Hermitage, producing the full-bodied red and delicate white Hermitage wines. There is a small harbour here and good shops.	77
LOCK BOURG-LES-VALENCE	105	1		
	108		**Valence** (pop: 55 000). Prosperous old town with many interesting historical associations. 11th C cathedral. You can moor by the bridge but there is also a fine marina at K112 and nearby supermarket.	77
LOCK BEAUCHASTEL	124	1		
LOCK DE BAIX-LOGIS-NEUF	142	1		
LOCK CHATEAUNEUF-DU-RHONE	164 166	1	**Viviers** A fascinating old town; just up the old Rhône. A rather rough quay and a tiny, unsuitable harbour.	
LOCK BOLLENE, DE ST PIERRE	187	1	**Bollène** (pop: 9000). An old tarn once owned by the monks of Avignon, with remains of 14th C defences. Tree-lined promenades and some fine houses indicate former splendour. Many new industries	80

Navigations	Km Mk	Locks	Towns and Villages	Michelin Map No
LOCK BOLLENE, DE ST PIERRE			are flourishing now. Bollène lies on the Donzère-Mondragon Canal, built in 1948–52 as part of a plan to regulate the Rhône and utilize it as a source of hydro-electric power. The André Blondel Usine-Barrage is the largest in Western Europe. From Bollène extends the southern region of the Côtes-du-Rhône; the vineyards are located east of Orange and on both sides of the Rhône.	
LOCK DE CADEROUSSE	216	1		
	224		**Roquemaure** Opposite is Chateauneuf-du-Pape where the noted wines of that name are produced; heir to the wines used by the Popes for Mass (14th C). Beyond Roquemaure are the villages of Tavel and Lirac. Quay.	80
LOCK D'AVIGNON	234	1		
	244		Turn back up to: **Avignon** (pop: 91 000). Great art town, most interesting and well known as the temporary residence of the Popes. The Palace of the Popes was built 1335–67, on a hill overlooking the town and the Pont d'Avignon of nursery rhyme fame. Museums: antiques, pictures. Across the river is Villeneuve-les-Avignon, summer residence of Popes. Good mooring but rather a noisy berth on the quay.	80, 83
	247		Turn back up to Port de Plaisance at: **La Courtine.** There are quayside fuel pumps here. If you draw more than 1.60 m look out for the bar at the entrance to the Durance.	

Navigations	Km Mk	Locks	Towns and Villages	Michelin Map No
LOCK DE TARASCON	265	1	**Tarascon** (Pop: 8500). Attractive old town, opposite Beaucaire. Castle of Tarascon, 14th C, prominent. No moorings here.	
Turn to STARBOARD *down the Petit Rhône if proceeding* WEST *(See Route 2)*	279			
	283		**Arles** (pop: 50 000). An ancient town, a capital city in Roman times with many important Roman and medieval buildings. Roman theatre, amphitheatre, alyscamps, necropolis. The forum, on the site of the Roman forum, is still the town centre. The best place to secure is in the basin through the lock; to reach it proceed down the Rhône for almost a kilometre and turn back up, through the lock, to Arles. There is a boatyard here.	83

The big lock just below Arles, leading only to moorings and the boatyard beyond. The lock gates are automatically operated from the upper storey of the building on the left.

The big lock at Port St Louis.

Route 12A
Arles to Port St Louis

Distance: **39 km (24 M)**   Number of Locks: **1**   Minimum height above water: **0**
Minimum depth of water: **1.45 m**

Navigations	Km Mk	Locks	Towns and Villages	Michelin Map No
RIVER RHONE	284		**Arles** (see page 144).	83
Turn back up LEFT *through 140° to enter into the* **ST LOUIS CANAL**	323	1	**Port St Louis** Small port beyond which are the sights, sounds and smells of heavy industry. At the boatyard the service is most helpful. There is a crane available for stepping/unstepping masts, also water on the quay, ample quayside mooring and shops nearby. A splendid place to pause and reflect.	84

Entry channel from the Rhône to Port St Louis.

Route 13
Messein to St Jean-de-Losne

Distance: **292 km (181 M)**   Number of locks: **106**   Minimum height above water: **3.45 m**
Minimum depth of water: **2.03 m**

Navigations	Km Mk	Locks	Towns and Villages	Michelin Map No
CANAL DE L'EST			**Messein** Shops and fuel available. Quay.	62
		5		
	13		**Crevechamps** Quay.	62
		10		
	19		**Charmes** Moorings and shops.	62
		6		
	10		**Nomexy** Quay. Village.	62
		5		
	8		**Thaon-les-Vosges** Fuel and shops. Quay.	62
LEFT *to Epinal* RIGHT *continue* CANAL DE L'EST	8		**Epinal** (pop: 35 000). Noted for cotton weaving and lace making. Fine park on Castle Hill. Church: St Maurice, 14th C. Museum: antiquities, pictures, and collection of Images d'Epinal.	62
		18		
	11		**Chaumousey** Quayside mooring. Note large number of locks from here.	62
		17		
	18		**Uzemain** Quay.	62
		11		
	12		**Bains-les-Bains** Quay.	62
		6		
	6		**Fontenoy-le-Château** Yacht harbour and charter craft.	62
		6		
	12		**Selles** Basin.	62
		4		
	9		**Corre** Pleasant stop with shops. Quay and charter craft.	62, 66
RIGHT *to* RIVER SAONE				
	3		**Ormoy**	66
		2		

Navigations	Km	Locks	Towns and Villages	Michelin Map No
Tunnel	16		**Montureux-les-Baulay**	66
RIVER SAONE		2		
	10		**Conflandey**	66
	8		**Port-sur-Saône** Moorings, shops and restaurants. Basin. Charter craft.	66
	10			
		1		
	2		**Chantes** Village.	66
		3		
	13		**Ray-sur-Saône** Attractive place with supermarket.	66
	10		**Savoyeaux** Marina and hire craft.	66
		4		
	26		**Gray** (pop: 8000). Market town in pretty setting. 15th C church; 16th C town hall. Good shops and facilities. Quays.	66
		1		
	24		**Heuilley-sur-Saône**	66
RIGHT **CANAL DE LA MARNE A LA SAONE**	2			
		1		
	3		**Pontailler-sur-Saône** Good shops, moorings and restaurants.	66
	16		**Auxonne**	66
		1		
LEFT **CANAL DU RHONE AU RHIN** RIGHT **CANAL DE BOURGOGNE**	13		**St Jean-de-Losne** Large basin with all facilities. Hire cruiser base.	66

Route 14
Paris to Condé

Distance: **180 km (111 M)**   Number of Locks: **16**   Minimum height above water: **3.79 m**
Miniumum depth of water: **2.18 m**

Navigations	Km	Locks	Towns and Villages	Michelin Map No
RIVER SEINE *after Pont de Conflans and just before Pont d'Ivry-s-Seine. Turn* LEFT *into* **RIVER**			**Paris** (See page 129)	56
MARNE	3			
Tunnel		2		
	2		**Joinville**	56
		2		
	23		**Lagny** Quay, town centre.	56
Tunnel	6			
		1		
RIGHT *Canal de Meaux à Chalifert*	11		**Meaux** Market town, capital of the Brie. Episcopal palace, 12th–17th C. Bossuet museum.	56
	11		**Germigny l'Eveque**	56
		1		
	11		**Mary-sur-Marne** Moorings.	56
		1		
	11		**St Jean-les-deux-Jumeaux** Club moorings and facilities.	56
	8		**La Ferte** Moorings.	56
		1		
	13		**Saacy**	56
		2		
	10		**Charly** Commercial quay.	56
		1		
	10		**Azy**	56
		1		

Navigations	Km	Locks	Towns and Villages	Michelin Map No
RIVER MARNE	6		Château-Thierry (pop: 11 000). Named after the castle built for King Thierry IV. Saw much action in both world wars. Nearby American National Cemetery of Bois-Belleau. Situated amidst wooded countryside. La Fontaine born here. Quay.	56
		2		
	24		Dormans Pretty little market town. Quay and shops.	56
		1		
	13		Port à Binson Commercial harbour.	56
		1		
	11		Cumières Quay. Village.	56
Junction to Epernay			Epernay (pop: 25 000). Main centre for the production and export of champagne. The miles of cellars and Champagne Museum, Musée du Vin de Champagne in Château Perrier, Avenue de Champagne, are well worth a visit. Pleasant town, Haut-villers Abbey known as the 'cradle of champagne' because it was here that Dom Pérignon first perfected the making of champagne. There is a memorial to him in the abbey ruins. The following champagne cellars can be visited: Moët et Chandon, Mercier (guided tour in model railway), De Castellane, G H Martel, Perrier-Jouet, Pol Roger. Wine tasting. Details from Syndicat d'Initiative.	56
	2		Ay Possesses long historic links with wine making including a half-timbered building known as Henri IV's wine press. The following champagne cellars can be visited: Ayala, 2 Boulevard du Nord (Mon–Fri); Bollinger, 16 Rue Jules Lobert (Mon–Fri, except August).	56

Navigations	Km	Locks	Towns and Villages	Michelin Map No
RIVER MARNE	5		**Condé-sur-Marne** Basin.	56

LEFT CANAL DE
L'AISNE A LA
MARNE
STRAIGHT ON *to*
CANAL
LATERAL A LA
MARNE

Route 15
Paris to St Mammes

Distance: **82 km (51 M)**   Number of locks: **8**   Minimum height above water: **5.79 m**
Minimum depth of water: **1.98 m**

Navigations	Km	Locks	Towns and Villages	Michelin Map No
RIVER SEINE			**Paris** (See page 129)	61
		1		
	11		**Villeneuve St Georges** (Orly airport on right.) Commercial quay.	61
		2		
	18		**Corbeil** Commercial quay.	61
		2		
	26		**Melun** (pop: 27 000). Capital of Seine et Marne; by the Forest of Fontainbleau. Notre-Dame church, 11th C. Quay.	61
		3		
RIGHT *into* **CANAL DU LOING**	27		**St Mammes** Junction for barge traffic. Quays.	61

St Mammes. Left, the Seine; right, Canal du Loing.

Route 16
St Mammes to Chalon-sur-Saône

Distance: **371 km (230 M)** Number of locks: **144** Minimum height above water: **3.66 m**
Minimum depth of water: **1.96 m**

Navigations	Km	Locks	Towns and Villages	Michelin Map No
CANAL DU LOING			**St Mammes**	61
		2		
	2		**Moret-sur-Loing** Small town. Pleasant old houses. Interesting place to stop.	
		5		
	19		**Nemours** Pleasant town in wooded setting. Museum. Quay.	61
		3		
	10		**Souppes-sur-Loing** Good shops. Basin.	61
		3		
	8		**Nargis** Shops and restaurants. Quay.	61
		3		
	6		**Cepoy** Quay.	61
		1		
RIGHT *Canal d'Orléans*	3		**Buges**	61
		4		
STRAIGHT ON *Canal de Briare*	5		**Montargis** (pop: 17 000). Picturesque old town. Good fishing area. Madeleine Church, 12th C. Moorings, shops and market. Basin.	61, 65
		6		
	11		**Montcresson** Quay.	65
	6		**Montbuoy** Quay.	65
		2		
	6		**Chatillon-Coligny** Convenient shops. Quay. Charter craft.	65
		6		
	10		**Rogny** Basin. Charter craft.	65
		12		
	11		**Ouzouer-sur-Trezee** Quay.	65

Navigations	Km	Locks	Towns and Villages	Michelin Map No
CANAL LATERAL A LA LOIRE	5		**Briare** (pop: 4000). Small town. Principal claim to fame is the Pont Canal, 640 m long, built by Eiffel in 1890 to carry the Briare Canal over the River Loire. Harbour	65
	8		**Chatillon-sur-Loire** Basin. Charter craft.	65
	6		**Beaulieu** Shops nearby. Basin.	65
		2		
	10		**Lere** Village.	65
		3		
	11		**Bannay**	65
	5		**Sancerre** (pop: 3000). Wine region. Noted for Sancerre, Pouilly-Fumé, Menetou-Salon, Pouilly-sur-Loire, and the VDQS St Pourcain-sur-Sioule. Tasting at Cave Cooperative, Avenue de Verdun.	65
		3		
	13		**Herry** Shops and water available. Basin.	65
		2		
	4		**Marseilles-les-Aubigny** Basin. Charter craft.	65, 69
Junction with Givry-Fourchamboult branch.	6			
Junction with Lorrains branch.	7	9	**Plagny** Basin. Charter craft.	69
Junction with Nevers branch.	1		**Nevers** (pop: 44 000). An interesting old town with medieval streets, chief town of the department of Nievre. Well known for pottery, the oldest of the earthenware factories was founded in 1648. Cathedral of St Cyr, 11th C; St Etienne church, 11th C; Ducal Palace, 15th C. Chapel of St Gildard's Convent contains the body of St Bernadette of Lourdes who died at Nevers	69

Navigations	Km	Locks	Towns and Villages	Michelin Map No
CANAL LATÉRAL A LA LOIRE			in 1879. Museum with typical specimens of French and other faiences, also valuable assortment of enamels.	
	9		**Chevenon** Village.	69
		4		
LEFT *junction to Decize*	25			
			Decize Basin. Charter craft.	69
		4		
	16		**Gannay** Basin. Charter craft.	69
		6		
	25		**Diou**	69
		3		
	11		**Coulanges** Village.	69
RIGHT *Canal de Roanne à Digoin*		1		
	8			
		1		
CANAL DU CENTRE	3		**Digoin** (pop: 8000). Industrial town, well known for pottery. Pont-Canal with eleven arches connects Canal latéral à la Loire with Canal du Centre. Basin. Charter craft.	69
		3		
	11		**Paray-le-Monial** Quay. Town.	69
		6		
	16		**Palinges** Quay.	69
		8		
	21		**Montceau-les-Mines** (pop: 30 000). Mining town. Nearby Le Creusot is the centre of coalfields and heavy industry. Basin.	69
		9		
	13		**Montchanin** Charter craft near.	69
		15		
	13		**St Berain-sur-Dheune** Quay.	69
		6		
	10		**St Gilles** Quay.	69

Navigations	Km	Locks	Towns and Villages	Michelin Map No
CANAL DU CENTRE	3		**Santenay** Quay.	69
	6		**Chagny** (pop: 5000). Thriving town between River Dheune and the canal. There are many of the famous Burgundy vineyards nearby: Chassagne-Montrachet, Puligny-Montrachet, Meursault (tasting at La Maison de Meursault), Monthélie (tasting at Caves de Monthélie), Volnay (tasting at Caveau de Monsieur Boillot), Pommard. Beaune, 16 km away and one of the most famous wine growing centres, is well worth a visit. Basin.	69
		12		
	18		**Chalon-sur-Saône** (pop: 46 000). Inland port and naval dockyard. Industrial and commercial town; canal boats built here. Centre of wine-growing district of Burgundy, the Côte Chalonnaise producing rich, fragrant red wines (Mercurey, Givry) and the fresh, clear whites (Rully, Montagny). Fine old houses. Marina and all facilities.	69
Junction **RIVER SAONE**				

Route 17
St Mammes to St Jean-de-Losne

Distance: **329 km (243 M)**   Number of Locks: **209**   Minimum height above water: **3.38 m**
Minimum depth of water: **1.96 m**

Navigations	Km	Locks	Towns and Villages	Michelin Map No
RIVER SEINE			**St Mammes**	61
		1		
RIGHT *into River Yonne* *(Petite Seine has been enlarged to Nogent)*	13		**Montereau** (pop: 10 000). Industrial town. Many barges there.	61
		5		
	32		**Pont-sur-Yonne** (pop: 2000). Pleasant small town. Old bridge and historical remains. 12th C Church. Quay. Charter craft.	61
		2		
	11		**Sens** (pop: 27 000). Old town with cathedral begun in 1140, one of the greatest Gothic buildings, magnificent stained-glass windows, treasury collection among the best known in Europe; lapidary museum in 13th C Synodal Palace. The Cathedral of St Etienne has relics of Thomas à Becket and his liturgical vestments. Yacht harbour.	61
		4		
	19		**Villeneuve-sur-Yonne** Interesting town. Old Royal residence. Quay. Charter craft.	61
		3		
	18		**Joigny** (pop: 8000). A pleasant little town, well known for its wine. Winding streets with half-timbered houses of 13th, 15th and 16th C. The arched bridge is 18th C. Riverside promenade. Churches: St Thibault, 15th C; St André, 11th C. Convenient quays to nearby shops. Charter craft.	61, 65

Navigations	Km	Locks	Towns and Villages	Michelin Map No
LEFT *into* **CANAL DE BOURGOGNE**	6	2	**Laroche** Small town. Railway centre. Basin 1 nearby shops.	65
	18	5	**St Florentin** (pop: 5000). Interesting little town, popular for fishing holidays. Noted for special cheese. Basin.	65
	13	7	**Flogny** Good shops. Moorings.	65
	13	4	**Tonnerre** (pop: 6000). Old town. Wine centre. 13th C hospital with arched wooden roof contains 15th C Holy Sepulchre, one of the best Burgundian statues to survive. Notre-Dame Church, 13th C.	65
	29	15	**Ancy-le-Libre** Basin.	65
	5	9	**Ravières** Basin.	65
	19	11	**Montbard** (pop: 6000). Industrial town in pretty setting. The celebrated naturalist, Buffon, was born in Montbard and it was here that he wrote his *Natural History*; near the ruined castle in the Parc de Buffon. Basin, shops near. Marina. Charter craft.	65
	13	9	**Venarey** Nearby Château de Bussy with interesting portraits. Quay. Charter craft.	65
	6	10	**Pouillenay** Basin.	65
	6	20	**Marigny-le-Cahouet** Basin.	65
	8	11	**Braux** Basin.	65
	10	2	**Beurizot** Basin.	65
		12		

Navigations	Km	Locks	Towns and Villages	Michelin Map No
CANAL DE BOURGOGNE	11		**Pouilley-en-Auxois** (pop: 1000). Small town by the Canal Tunnel. Notre-Dame Church, 14th C. Basin some way from town. Charter craft.	65
Tunnel		16		
	13		**Crugey** Basin.	65
		16		
	16		**Gissey-sur-Ouche** Basin.	65, 66
		13		
	13		**Verlars-sur-Ouche** Shops nearby. Quay.	65, 66
		9		
	11		**Dijon** (pop: 140 000) Old medieval, industrial and wine trading city. Flourishing commercial and art centre. Many reminders that in the 15th C Dijon was a chief centre of European civilization. Cathedral: St Benigne, 13th C Church of Notre-Dame with celebrated Jack-o-the-clock. Palais de Justice, former seat of the Burgundy Parlement. Fine arts museum houses one of the oldest and best art galleries in France. Several other museums, Fragonard, Latour, Manet. From Dijon to Santenay (near to Chagny), is the Côte d'Or, the biggest wine-producing district of Burgundy. In the 24 km (15 M) from Dijon to Nuits St George are the estates of Marsanny-La-Cote, Gevrey-Chambertin (tasting in 17th C vaulted cellars of Maison Thomas Bassot), Chambolle-Musigny, Clos De Vougeot, Vosnee-Romanée. Basin near Shops. Harbour. Charter craft.	65, 66
		16		
	15		**Longecourt-en-Plane** Basin.	65, 66
		7		

Navigations	Km	Locks	Towns and Villages	Michelin Map No
CANAL DE BOURGOGNE *Junction with River Saône*	13		**St Jean-de-Losne** Important in view of its position as a waterway junction of the Doubs and Saône rivers and the Burgundy, Centre and Rhône-Rhine canals. Harbour. Dry dock. Charter craft.	

St Jean-de-Losne. Lock and basin beyond. The barge has just entered from the Saône.

The Brittany canals

In view of the restoration work done in recent years, the Brittany canals deserve a mention, linking in, as they do with the Route 18 St Nazaire to St Malo route. If you find yourself in your boat in this part of France it is certainly worthwhile indulging in a little extra exploration. You can also charter cruisers from many hire companies in Brittany. The French Government Tourist Office will send you the current brochure, *Tourisme fluvial en Bretagne*.

Rohan.

Josselin.

The route from St Nazaire, through Nantes, Redon and
Rennes to St Malo is covered in Route 18, plus a mention of the
diversion from Redon to the sea at La Roche Bernard. The
other Brittany canals are the continuation of the Canal de
Nantes à Brest, north from Redon. The section from Rohan to
Carhaix has been closed for many years so that it is not possible
to cruise all the way to Brest. The section from Rohan to
Pontivy has been opened up, somewhat intimidating with 54
locks in 24 kms (38 M). At Pontivy the Canal du Blavet joins up
with the River Blavet enabling you to cruise to Lorient and the
sea again.

Navigations	Km	Locks	Towns and Villages	Michelin Map No
CANAL DE NANTES A BREST			**Redon** Noted for its splendid grouping of waterways and locks.	
		7		
	38		**Malestroit** Quay. Unusual carvings on the houses are worth inspection.	
		10		
	25		**Josselin** Quay. Hire cruiser base. The imposing Château Josselin is alongside the waterway. See the collection of dolls in the Musée des Poupées.	
		16		
	24		**Rohan** A cruiser base. Back along the towpath is the Cistercian Abbaie de Timadeuc where you may attend mass.	
		55		
	24		**Pontivy** Market town, twisting streets.	
CANAL DU BLAVET		28		
	59		**Hennebont** An old walled town.	
RIVER BLAVET	11		**Lorient.**	

Route 18
St Nazaire to St Malo

Route A to Redon
Distance: **109 km (175 M)**   Number of Locks: **9**   Minimum height above water:
3.66 m   Minimum depth of water: **1.52 m**
Route B to Redon (coastal passage to the River Vilaine)
Distance (from La Roche Bernard): **39 km (62 M)** to Redon
Number of locks: **1**   Minimum depth of water: **1.22 m**

Navigations	Km	Locks	Towns and Villages	Michelin Map No
Route A to Redon				
RIVER LOIRE			**St Nazaire** (pop: 60 000). Commercial and shipbuilding town with dockyards and harbour prominent. Greatly damaged in World War II, much of it by the Royal Navy attacking the German U-boat base.	67
	8		**Paimboeuf** Quay.	67
	40		**Nantes** (pop: 250 000). Modern industrial town and commercial seaport. Chief claim to fame, the Edict of Nantes issued by Henry IV of France granting Protestants liberty of worship and equal political rights with Roman Catholics. Ducal Château, 14th C (in which Edict was signed). Museums: fine arts, archaeology, art, history of Nantes, and marine history of Nantes. Cathedral: St Pierre, 15th C. Le Corbusier's new housing estate (Cité Radieuse) is just across the river at Rezé-les-Nantes. The vineyards of the Loire Valley are divided into four separate areas. Nearest to the sea are the wines of the region of Nantes. Then Anjou and Saumur and, further inland, Touraine and	67

Port de Plaisance La Roche Bernard.

Redon: Canal de Nantes à Brest crossing the River Vilaine.

Navigations	Km	Locks	Towns and Villages	Michelin Map No
			Sancerre. Muscadet is produced in the Nantes region, a light white wine, very fruity. Wine tasting at Caveau de Nantes, 17 Rue des Etats.	
LEFT *into* **RIVER ERDRE**	13		**Suce**	63
	6			
LEFT *into* **CANAL DE NANTES A BREST**	13		**La Chevallerais** Quay.	63
		3		
	8		**Blain** Moorings and restaurants.	63
		5		
	22		**Guenrouet** Quay.	63
		1		
	22		**Redon** (pop: 14 000). Small market town with some industry. Because of the silting of the River Vilaine, Redon has been cut off from the sea and port activity has decreased. The construction of a maritime lock at Arzal and the dredging of the bed of the Vilaine will enable marine traffic to use the port of Redon again. Church: St Sauveur, 12th C.	63

Route B to Redon

From St Nazaire coastal passage **36 km (58 M)** to River Vilaine (see Admiralty Chart No 2353).

Navigations	Km	Locks	Towns and Villages	Michelin Map No
RIVER VILAINE			**La Roche Bernard** There is a marina in this pleasant town.	63
		1		
CANAL DE NANTES A BREST	29			
	10		**Redon** (by this route a mast need not be unstepped until Redon).	63

Dinan. Pleasant waterside restaurants. Masts down if continuing south.

Navigations	Km	Locks	Towns and Villages	Michelin Map No

Redon to St Malo

Distance: **199 km (320 M)**   Number of locks: **60**   Minimum height above water: **2.26 m**
Minimum depth of water: **1.22 m**

Navigations	Km	Locks	Towns and Villages	Michelin Map No
RIGHT *into* **RIVER VILAINE**			**Redon**	63
	27		**Port de Roche** Quay.	
		2		
	14		**Messac** Charter cruisers depot, moorings and fuel.	63
		6		
	30		**Pont Rean** Quay. Charter craft.	63
		5		
	18		**Rennes** (pop: 190 000). Industrial and agricultural centre. Capital of the department of Ile-et-Vilaine. Palais de Justice, 17th C. Cathedral, 19th C. Museum: Latour, Poussin. Port du Mail.	63, 59
LEFT *into* **CANAL D'ILLE ET RANCE**		6		
	13		**Betton** Moorings. Charter craft.	59
		4		
	10		**St Germain-sur-Ille** Quay.	59
		6		
	10		**Montreuil-sur-Ille** Quay.	59
		16		
	16		**Tinteniac** Several restaurants here. Quay.	59
		7		
	13		**Treverien** Quay.	59
		1		
	6		**Evran** Quay.	59
		5		
	11		**Dinan** (pop: 18 000). Old walled town. Quaint streets and picturesque houses. 14th C castle. Church: St Sauveur, 14th C. Harbour.	59
		1		

Navigations	Km	Locks	Towns and Villages	Michelin Map No
RIVER RANCE			La Vicomte	59
	31		St Malo (pop: 47 000). Attractive and historic seaport; with its town walls it resembles a medieval fortress. Derives its name from a Welsh monk. Much damaged in World War II and rebuilt on original lines. Castle: 14th C. Church: St Vincent, 13th C.	59

Route 19
St Valéry to St Simon

Distance: **160 km (99 M)**   Number of locks: **22**   Minimum height above water: **3.45 m**
Minimum depth of water: **1.70 m**

Navigations	Km	Locks	Towns and Villages	Michelin Map No
CANAL DE LA SOMME			St Valéry-sur-Somme (pop: 3000). Pleasantly situated little holiday resort, an ancient town with ramparts and fortified gates. Upstream from the town are berths at the Sport Nautique. The lock into the Canal de la Somme is beyond the Yacht Club.	52
		2		
	16		Abbeville (pop: 23 000). Largely rebuilt following air raids of World War II. Belonged to England for 200 years from 1272 on marriage of Edward I to Eleanor of Castile. Museum: ceramics, paintings; collection of wild fowl of the Somme valley.	52
		1		
	10		Pont-Remy Pleasant mooring.	52
		3		
	23		Picquigny Village.	52, 53
		3		
	16		Amiens (pop: 131 000). Ancient capital of Picardy, now of the department of Somme. Headquarters of the British Army in World War I. Largely destroyed in World War II and rebuilt on modern lines. World famous textile centre for manufacture of velvet. Cathedral of Notre-Dame is the largest in France (completed 1269) and one of the greatest architectural creations in the world. Museum: rich collection of paintings, Bonnard, Fragonard, Gauguin, Matisse. Water market of boats selling fruit and vegetables. Quay. Charter craft.	52, 53

Navigations	Km	Locks	Towns and Villages	Michelin Map No
CANAL DE LA SOMME		2		
	16		**Corbie** Shops and moorings.	52, 53
		2		
	11		**Chipilly** Quay.	52, 53
		2		
	10		**Froissy** Quay.	52, 53
		1		
Left *Canal du Nord*	16			
	3		**Péronne** (pop: 7000). Almost completely rebuilt following war damage; featured in the Battle of the Somme. Two museums. Church: St John, 1520.	52, 53
		1		
	11		**St Christ** Quay.	52, 53
		1		
	5		**Pargny** Quay.	52, 53
Right *Canal du Nord*	8		**Voyennes**	52, 53
		3		
	9		**Ham** Basin. Village.	53
		1		
	6		**St Simon**	53
Junction with Canal de Saint-Quentin				

Route 20
Strasbourg to Chalon-sur-Saône

Distance: **408 km (253 M)**   Number of locks: **134**   Minimum height above water: **3.48 m**
Minimum depth of water: **1.98 m**

Navigations	Km	Locks	Towns and Villages	Michelin Map No
RIVER RHINE			Strasbourg (See page 179).	87
		2		
	30		**Rhinau**	87
		2		
	22	1	**Marckolsheim**	87
	14		**Breisach** Yacht harbour. To the west of the Canal du Rhône au Rhin, from Strasbourg to Mulhouse, are 45 000 acres of vineyards dating back to Roman times. La Route du Vin d'Alsace is, in fact, from Wangen to Thann, and the most convenient point near the waterway from which to visit this wine area is Colmar. Among the great wines to have made Alsace famous are Sylvander, Riesling, Pinot Blanc, Gewürztraminer, Tokay, the Muscatels, and Zwicker.	87
Right *Canal de Colmar* **GRAND CANAL D'ALSACE**	1		**Colmar** (pop: 62 000). One of the most attractive old towns in Alsace. Many fine old wooden houses of the 16th–17th C. Cathedral: 13th C; Dominican's church: 13th C. Wine capital of Alsace, retaining the aspect of an old Alsatian town. The Unterlinden museum contains a reconstructed Alsatian wine cellar and wine museum, also the Isenheim altarpiece by Mathias Grünewald, one of the world's greatest paintings. From Colmar there are coach excursions to La Route du Vin d'Alsace.	87

Navigations	Km	Locks	Towns and Villages	Michelin Map No
CANAL DU RHONE AU RHIN	41	4		
Left *Canal de Huningue to Swiss frontier*	13	5	**Mulhouse** (pop: 120 000). Industrial town, largest in the Upper Rhine Department; spinning and weaving. Was German town for fifty years up to 1918. Town Hall built in 1552; Chapel of St Jean, former possession of the Knights of Malta. Museum of weaving and textiles. Large zoo. Quayside moorings.	87, 66
	6	5	**Zillisheim** Village.	87, 66
	11	12	**Hagenbach** Quay.	87, 66
	22	21	**Montreux** Basin. Village nearby.	87, 66
	10	3	**Froidefontaine** Village.	87, 66
		8		

Between Clerval and Baume-les-Dames.

Navigations	Km	Locks	Towns and Villages	Michelin Map No
CANAL DU RHONE AU RHIN	13		**Montbeliard** (pop: 20 000). Industrial town. 18th C Château des Princes, now a museum, overlooks the town. Quaint old houses. Yacht harbour.	87, 66
		6		
	8		**Colombier-Fontaine** Shops and nearby fuel. Commercial quay.	66
		6		
	13		**L'Isle-sur-le-Doubs** Basin. Town nearby.	66
		6		
	13		**Clerval** Moorings.	66
		7		
	16		**Baume-les-Dames** (pop: 5000). Ancient town, named after a nunnery that was once on the site. Many 18th C houses. Nearby supermarket. Yacht facilities.	66
		12		
	29		**Laissey**	66
		4		
	21		**Besançon** (pop: 100 000). Important town, centre of the French watchmaking industry, also artificial silk. Palais de Justice, 16th C; once meeting place of the Franche-Comté. Birthplace of Victor Hugo, also Lumière brothers, inventors of the moving picture. Museum contains interesting watch and clock section. Many gracious buildings. Fuel available. Yacht facilities.	66
		4		
	14			
Tunnel		5		
	17		**Fraisans** Village.	66
		7		
	23		**Dole** (pop: 28 000). Old town, ancient capital of Franche-Comté. Rich in history and architecture of 16th, 17th, and 18th C.	66, 70

Navigations	Km	Locks	Towns and Villages	Michelin Map No
CANAL DU RHONE AU RHIN			Five museums. The vineyards of Arbois, 30 km (18 M) away to the East, are the first to be given *Appellation Contrôlée* by the French Government. The wines produced around Arbois, in the Jura foothills, are white, red, and rosé. The great names of the Jura vineyards are Arbois, Etoile, Château Chalon, and Côtes du Jura. Yacht harbour and good shops.	
		9		
	18		**St Symphorien** (pop: 2000). Busy canal junction.	70
LEFT *into River Saône*				
	3		**St Jean-de-Losne**	70
RIGHT *Canal de Bourgogne*				
		1		
	15		**Seurre** (pop: 2000). Pleasant old town.	70
		2		
LEFT *River Doubs*	9		**Verdun-sur-el-Doubs** Restaurants offer fish speciality.	70
From RIGHT *Canal de centre*	24			
	2		**Chalon-sur-Saône**	70

Route 21
Toul to Strasbourg
via Frouard

Distance: **193 km (119 M)**   Number of locks: **62**   Minimum height above water: **3.68 m**
Minimum depth of water: **2.18 m**

Navigations	Km	Locks	Towns and Villages	Michelin Map No
CANALIZED RIVER MOSELLE			**Toul** (See page 182)	62
		3		
	20		**Liverdun** Attractive medieval town.	62
		1		
CANAL DE LA MARNE AU RIIIN	6		**Frouard** Town of heavy industry.	62
	10		**Nancy** (pop: 150 000). Capital of Lorraine in the heart of an important industrial region. Old university town. Fine example of baroque town planning, much of which remains. Magnificent public squares, largest, Place Stanislas, surrounded by palaces. Ducal Palace, 16th C. Five museums with Delacroix, Manet. Basin.	62
		1		
RIGHT *Canal de l'Est*	6		**Laneuville-Devant-Nancy** Basin.	62
		2		
	7		**Varangeville** Quay.	62
		6		
	13		**Einville** Basin.	62
		3		
	13		**Xures** Basin.	62
		5		
	11		**Moussey** Basin.	62
LEFT *Canal des Houilleres de la Sarre to German frontier*		6		
	14		**Gondrexange**	62, 87
	4		**Heming**	62, 87

Navigations	Km	Locks	Towns and Villages	Michelin Map No
CANAL DE LA MARNE AU RHIN	8		**Hesse** Wide basin, hire cruisers and all facilities.	87, 62
Tunnel	10			
	14		Inclined Plane St Louis-Arzviller.	
		5		
	4		**Lutzelbourg** A beautiful town. Basin. Charter craft.	87, 62
		9		
	10		**Saverne** A splendid town with good shops. Basin.	87, 62
		15		

The inclined plane, St Louis-Arzviller. *Photo Karquel*

Châlons-sur-Marne. Canal latéral à la Marne. *Photo Yan*

Navigations	Km	Locks	Towns and Villages	Michelin Map No
CANAL DE LA MARNE AU RHIN	8		Dettwiller	87
		7		
	13		**Waltenheim-s-Zorn** Quay.	87
		5		
	11		**Vendenheim**	87
		4		
	11		**Strasbourg** (pop: 250 000). Capital of the department of Bas-Rhin. Important river port, commercial and cultural centre. Belonged to France and Germany in turn, became French again in 1918. Both architectural influences are apparent. Much damaged in World War II. Cathedral Notre-Dame: 12th C. Famous clock. Museums: furniture, domestic, also Corot, Fragonard, Watteau, Dégas, Monet, Renoir, Braque, Gauguin. Several club moorings available.	87

Route 22
Vitry-le-François to Messein

Distance: **156 km (96 M)**   Number of locks: **97**   Minimum height above water: **3.68 m**
Minimum depth of water: **2.18 m**

Navigations	Km	Locks	Towns and Villages	Michelin Map No
CANAL DE LA MARNE AU RHIN			**Vitry-le-François** A barge town with all facilities.	61
LEFT *Canal latéral à*		4		
la Saône	13		**Bignicourt** Quay.	61
		7		
	11		**Sermaize-les-Bains** Basin.	61
		13		
	13		**Mussey** Basin.	61, 65
		7		
	8		**Bar-le-Duc** (pop: 20 000). Industrial town, capital of the department of Meuse. Ancient houses. Church of St Etienne containing gruesome statue: (the skeleton of Prince René de Châlons, whose dying wish was that his tomb effigy should resemble his body three years after his death). Monument to Pierre and Ernest Michaux who invented the pedal cycle. Quay.	61, 62
		7		
	8		**Tannois** Quay. Village nearby.	62
		10		
	8		**Ligny-en-Barrois** Pleasant town. Basin.	62
		21		
	22		**Demange-aux-Eaux** Shops with supermarket nearby. Quay.	62
Tunnel		1		
	10		**Mauvages** Village nearby.	62
		12		
	10		**Void** Quay. Village.	62
LEFT *Canal de l'Est (Branch Nord)*	7		**Troussey**	62

Demange-aux-Eaux.

Yacht basin, Toul.

Navigations	Km	Locks	Towns and Villages	Michelin Map No
Tunnel	10			
		13		
CANALIZED MOSELLE	10		**Toul** (pop: 14 000). Old fortified town. Tourist centre of Lorraine. Ancient ramparts and twin-towered cathedral, 13th C. Church: St Gengoult, 13th C. Joan of Arc once came to Toul. A young man from her village pretended that she had promised to marry him and indicted her before Henri de Ville, Bishop of Toul.	62
		3		
RIGHT _Canal de l'Est_	22		**Neuves-Maisons** There is a steel works here.	62
		2		
	2		**Messein** Quay. Village.	62

Route 23
Watten to Chauny

Distance: **205 km (127 M)**   Number of locks: **43**   Minimum height above water: **3.68 m**
Minimum depth of water: **2.18 m**

Navigations	Km	Locks	Towns and Villages	Michelin Map No
RIVER AA			**Watten** Quay.	51
DUNKERQUE-ESCAUT WATERWAY	10		**St Omer** (pop: 20 000). Centre of agriculture. Much damaged in both world wars. Notre-Dame, 13th C. Museum: fine arts, paintings include four of Breughel the Elder including the celebrated 'Surgical Operation'. Quay.	51
		2		
LEFT *Canal de la Nieppe to River Lys to Belgian frontier*	10		**Aire-sur-la-Lys** (pop: 10 000). On the river Lys and Canal d'Aire, 17th C town.	51
RIGHT *to Bethune*	20		**Bethune** (pop: 25 000). Industrial town with docks. Much damaged in both world wars. British cemetery of World War I at Neuve Chapelle, 9 km (5 M) away. Yacht harbour.	51, 53
		1		
	14		**La Bassee** Canal divides.	51, 53
		6		
LEFT *to Lille and Belgian frontier*			**Lille** (pop: 200 000). Big industrial town, one of the greatest textile centres in the world. Was once named l'Isle, thus Lisle thread which came from here. Birthplace of Général de Gaulle. Modern cathedral. Museum holds richest collection of art outside Paris with Goyas, Rubens, Franz Hals, Van Dyck, Veronese, Titian, Delacroix, Corot, Monet, Sisley, Renoir.	51, 53
	4		**Bauvin**	51, 53
	7		**Anway** Quay and basin.	51, 53

Navigations	Km	Locks	Towns and Villages	Michelin Map No
DUNKERQUE-ESCAUT WATERWAY				
RIGHT *Canal de Lens to Lens*	4		**Lens** (pop: 42 000). An industrial town in a mining area with long lines of slag heaps.	51, 53
LEFT *River Scarpe to Belgian frontier*	14			
RIGHT *to Arras*				
	2		**Doual** An important industrial centre in the heart of the coal basin. Quay.	51, 53
	5		**Ferin** Quay.	53
		1		
RIGHT *Canal du Nord*	7		**Arleux** Moorings and village.	53
	5		**Aubigny-au-Bac** Basin. Quay. Village nearby.	53
RIGHT *into River Escaut*		5		
LEFT *to Belgian frontier*				
CANAL DE SAINTE-QUENTIN	11		**Cambrai** (pop: 36 000). Prosperous town noted for weaving and fine linen cloth; 'cambric' invented here. Saw much action in World War I, tanks first used in Battle of Cambrai, November 1917. Much damage which was restored, destroyed again in World War II and restored again. Plenty of barge activity. Basin. Hire cruisers.	53
		4		
	6		**Marcoing** Quay. Village.	53
		2		

Arras on the River Scarpe. *Photo J. Feuillie*

Navigations	Km	Locks	Towns and Villages	Michelin Map No
CANAL DE SAINT-QUENTIN	3		**Masnières** Quays. Village.	53
		7		
	11		**Bantouzelle**	53
		4		
	6		**Vendhuile** Village. Basin.	53
Tunnel		2		
	16		**Lesdins** Village.	53

From the French canals it is easy to enter Belgian and Dutch waters such as the river Ling at Gelderland. *Photo L Philippe*

Navigations	Km	Locks	Towns and Villages	Michelin Map No
CANAL DE SAINT-QUENTIN	6	3	**St Quentin** (pop: 60 000). Industrial centre, textiles. Interesting town, rich in historical association. Fine Hôtel de Ville. Museum: works of Quentin de la Tour. Quay.	53
	7		**Fontaine-les-Clercs** Village.	53
		2		
	6		**Artemps** Village.	53
		1		
	2		**Tugny-et-Pont** Quays.	53
		1		
RIGHT *Canal de la Somme*	2		**St Simon** Village.	53
	6		**Jussy** Village.	53
		2		
	9		**Quessy** Quay. Village.	53, 56
		3		
	2		**Tergnier** Quay.	56
LEFT *to La Fère to join Canal de la Sambre à l'Oise to Landrecies and frontier*		4		
	8		**Chauny** (pop: 12 000). Industrial town.	56

From Belgium into France

Route BF/1
Furnes to Dunkirk

Distance: **22 km (13 M)**   Number of locks: **1**   Minimum height above water: **3.50 m**
Minimum depth of water: **1.80 m**   Maximum LOA: **40.40 m**   Maximum beam: **6 m**

Navigations	Km	Locks	Towns and Villages	Michelin Map No
CANAL DE NIEUWPOORT A DUNKERQUE			**Furnes** Attractive town. Small harbour.	
		1		
	4		**Adinkerke** The district is a place of pilgrimage to the many war cemeteries.	
FRONTIER				
Continue as Canal de Furnes	4		**Bray-Dunes**	51
	6		**Zuydcoote** Village.	51
	7		**Rosendael**	51
	1		**Dunkirk**	51

Route BF/2
Menin to Armentières

Distance: **51 km (31 M)**   Number of locks: **3**   Minimum height above water: **4 m**
Minimum depth of water: **1.90 m**   Maximum LOA: **42.32 m**   Maximum beam: **5.40 m**

Navigations	Km	Locks	Towns and Villages	Michelin Map No
RIVER LYS			**Menin**	
		1		
	4		**Wervik** (pop: 13 000).	
	7		**Comines** (pop: 9000). Industrial town.	
		1		
	6		**Warneton**	

From here the river is the frontier between Belgium and France for 25 km. Jointly owned.

FRONTIER

Navigations	Km	Locks	Towns and Villages	Michelin Map No
RIVER LYS	2		**Deulemont**	51
LEFT *Bauvin-Lys branch of Dunkerque-Escaut Waterway*	2		**Frelinghein**	51
		1		
	5		**Armentières** Yacht harbour nearby at Press Duhem.	51

Route BF/3

Antoing to Douai

Distance: **47 km (29 M)**   Number of Locks: **7**   Minimum height above water: **3.70 m**
Minimum depth of water: **2.10 m**   Maximum LOA: **38.50 m**   Maximum beam: **5.15 m**

Navigations	Km	Locks	Towns and Villages	Michelin Map No
RIVER ESCAUT			Antoing	
	6		Peronnes	
	4		Bleharies	
FRONTIER				
FROM LEFT *join* RIVER SCARPE	3	2	Mortagne du Nord	51
	11		St Amand-les-Eaux Quay.	51
	4	3	Warlaing Village.	51
	12	2	Lallaing Quay.	51
	7		Douai	51

Route BF/4
Antoing to Condé

Distance: **26 km (16 M)**   Number of Locks: **1**   Minimum height above water: **3.70 m**
Minimum depth of water: **2.10 m**   Maximum LOA: **38.50 m**   Maximum beam: **5.15 m**

Navigations	Km	Locks	Towns and Villages	Michelin Map No
RIVER ESCAUT			Antoing	
	6		Peronnes	
	4		Bleharies	
FRONTIER				
RIVER ESCAUT	3		Mortagne du Nord Moorings.	51
		1		
	7		Hergnies Village.	51
Junction CANAL POMMEROEUL-CONDE	6		Condé-sur-l'Escaut	51

Route BF/5
Blaton to Conde'

Distance: **11 km (7 M)**   Number of locks: **8**   Minimum height above water: **3.70 m**
Minimum depth of water: **1.80 m**   Maximum LOA: **38.50 m**   Maximum beam: **5.10 m**

Navigations	Km	Locks	Towns and Villages	Michelin Map No
CANAL DE POMMEROEUL A ANTOING			Blaton	
Junction Canal Nimy-Blaton				
		5		
RIGHT *into* CANAL DE POMMEROEUL A CONDE		1		
	8		Hensies	
FRONTIER				
CANAL DE POMMEROEUL A CONDE			St Aybert Village.	51
		2		
	3		Condé	51

Route BF/6
Charleroi to Maubeuge

Distance: **52 km (32 M)**   Number of Locks: **13**   Minimum height above water: **3.25 m**
Minimum depth of water: **1.90 m**   Maximum LOA: **38.50 m**   Maximum beam: **5.15 m**

Navigations	Km	Locks	Towns and Villages	Michelin Map No
RIVER SAMBRE			Charleroi	
From LEFT *Canal de*				
Charleroi à Bruxelles	2			
		2		
	5		**Montignies-le-Tilleul**	
		4		
	13		**Thuin** Pleasantly situated above the Sambre. Interesting historical associations include the base of the Tour Notger, a relic of the fortifications set up by the Bishop of that name around 1000 AD. Early 16th C abbey.	
		4		
	15		**Merbes-le-Château**	
		1		
	5		**Erquelinnes**	
FRONTIER				
RIVER SAMBRE			**Jeumont** Quay.	51
		2		
	12		**Maubeuge** Quays. Town nearby.	51

Route BF/7
Namur to Pont-a-Bar

Distance: **139 km (86 M)**   Number of locks: **28**   Minimum height above water: **3.70 m**
Minimum depth of water: **2.20 m**   Maximum LOA: **48.30 m**   Maximum beam: **5.70 m**

Navigations	Km	Locks	Towns and Villages	Michelin Map No
RIVER MEUSE			Namur	
		1		
	6		**Wepion** Attractive holiday centre, famous for strawberries. 'Strawberry Sunday' is the third in June.	
		1		
	6		**Profondeville** Pleasant spot, but rather crowded at weekends during summer.	
		1		
	5		**Godin**	
	2		**Yvoir**	
		1		
	5		**Anhee**	
		1		
	3		**Bouvignies** Pleasant little town with a number of old buildings well restored after destruction of World War I.	
		1		
	2		**Dinant** (pop: 10 000). Main tourist centre for the Belgian Ardennes and holiday resort on the river Meuse, situated beneath an almost vertical cliff. Pleasant town with a long acquaintance with war and sackings; in 1944 the Americans drove the Nazis from the citadel. Largely rebuilt. 13th C Notre-Dame church, with bulbous Baroque tower, Citadel with museum. Telesiege of Dinant takes you by chairlift to the tower of the Mont-Fat, 110 m above the River Meuse. *Syndicat d'Initiative*: Hôtel de Ville.	
	2		**Anseremme.** An attractive river resort.	

Navigations	Km	Locks	Towns and Villages	Michelin Map No
RIVER MEUSE		1		
	7		Waulsort	
		1		
	4		Hastiere-Lavaux	
		1		
	5		Heer	

Dinant.

Navigations	Km	Locks	Towns and Villages	Michelin Map No
FRONTIER				
CANAL DE L'EST NORTHERN BRANCH (RIVER MEUSE)	1		**Givet** Moorings.	53
		1		
Tunnel	3			
		3		
	7		**Vireux** Village.	53

The Moselle at Toul.

Navigations	Km	Locks	Towns and Villages	Michelin Map No
CANAL DE L'EST NORTHERN BRANCH (RIVER MEUSE)		3		
	13		**Fumay** Quay.	53
		3		
Tunnel	12		**Revin** Moorings.	53
		3		
	11		**Laifour** Quay.	53
		1		
	9		**Montherme** Small town.	53
		2		
	12		**Nouzonville** Quay.	53
		1		
	9		**Mezieres**	53
		1		
	6		**Lumes** Quay.	53
		1		
Junction Canal des Ardennes	9		**Pont-a-Bar**	53

From Germany and Luxembourg into France

Route GLF/1
Remerschen to Frouard
Distance: **100 km (62 M)**   Number of locks: **13**   Minimum height above water: **3.70 m**
Minimum depth of water: **2.60 m**   Maximum LOA: **39.60 m**   Maximum beam: **6 m**

The Moselle forms the frontier between Germany and the Grand Duchy of Luxembourg.

Navigations	Km	Locks	Towns and Villages	Michelin Map No
RIVER MOSELLE			Remerschen	
	2			
FRONTIER Right bank: Grand Duchy of Luxembourg Left bank: Germany				
	2		**Contz-les-Bains**	57
	7		**Malling**	57
		1		
	14		**Thionville** Quay near town.	57
		2		
	11		**Mondelange**	57
		2		
METZ DIVERSION CANAL	15		**Metz** (pop: 150 000). Ancient Gallic town that was fortified by the Romans.	57
		3		
Junction with Canal de Jouy à Metz	12		**Ancy-sur-Moselle**	57
	4		**Corny-sur-Moselle** Moorings.	57

Navigations	Km	Locks	Towns and Villages	Michelin Map No
		3		
	6		**Pagny-sur-Moselle** Basin. Charter craft.	57
	9		**Pont-a-Mousson** Quay. Charter craft.	57
		1		
	7		**Dieulouard**	57
	7		**Marbache**	57
		1		
	4		**Frouard**	57

From Germany into France

Route GF/2
Kleinblittersdorf to Gondrexange

Distance: **65 km (40 M)**   Number of locks: **27**   Minimum height above water: **3.65 m**
Minimum depth of water: **2.20 m**   Maximum LOA: **39 m**   Maximum beam: **5.20 m**

Navigations	Km	Locks	Towns and Villages	Michelin Map No
CANALIZED RIVER SAAR			Kleinblittersdorf	
FRONTIER				
CANAL DES HOUILLERES DE LA SARRE	11		**Sarreguemines** Quay in town.	57
		5		
	11		**Wittring** Quay. Village.	57
		3		
	11		**Sarralbe** Quay. Small town.	57
		2		
	12		**Harskirchen** Basin. Charter craft.	57
		4		
	9		**Mittersheim** Basin. Charter craft.	57
		13		
Junction Canal de la Marne au Rhin	11		**Gondrexange**	57

Route GF/3
Lauterbourg to Strasbourg
Distance: **56 km (35 M)**   Number of locks: 2   Minimum height above water: **7 m**
Minimum depth of water: **2.70 m**   Maximum LOA: **185 m**   Maximum beam: **23 m**

Navigations	Km	Locks	Towns and Villages	Michelin Map No
RIVER RHINE			**Lauterbourg** Harbour.	87
	9		**Seltz**	87
		1		
	20		**Drusenheim** Village.	87
		1		
	27		**Strasbourg**	87

The Rhine forms the frontier between France and Germany for 200 km (124 M), from the Swiss frontier at Basle to Lauterbourg.

From Basle south into France, the Canal de Huningue links (from Niffer to Mulhouse), with the Canal du Rhône au Rhin (see Route 20).

Selected bibliography

Books and charts on the inland waterways of France and the rest of Europe can be obtained by mail order from Warsash Nautical Bookshop 6 Dibles Rd, Warsash, Southampton SO3 9HZ (Tel 04895 72384). See also page 46.

General
Agenda du Marinier, annually, Editions de la Navigation du Rhin, Strasbourg. (Commercial boatman's diary, containing quantities of useful information, addresses and phone numbers of waterways authorities etc.)
Inland Waterways of France, David Edwards-May, 1991, Imray, Huntingdon. (Distance tables, locks, bridges etc for entire network.)
Cruising French Waterways, Hugh McKnight, 1991, Adlard Coles Nautical, London. (Descriptive guide to all French canals and rivers. Winner of the Thomas Cook Guide Book Award.)
Notes on French Inland Waterways, Vernon Marchant, 1993, Cruising Association, London. (Useful introduction with regulations, routes etc.)

Maps, Charts and Pilot Books
France Itineraires Fluviaux No 21 Editions Cartographiques Maritimes, Bagneux, France. (Large folding coloured map, showing locks, intermediate distances etc.)
Carte Guides, Editions Cartographiques Maritimes. (Contain highly detailed maps with all facilities, in English and French text, regularly updated.)

1 *La Seine* Le Havre – Paris

2 *La Seine* Paris – Head of Navigation

3 *La Marne* Paris – Vitry-le-François

4 *L'Yonne* Auxerre – Monterau

5 *Canal de Bourgogne* Yonne – Saône

6 *Canaux du Centre* Seine – Saône, via Loing, Briare, C latéral à la Loire, C du Centre and Roanne-Digoin Branch

7 *Canal du Nivernais* Decize – Auxerre

8 *Champagne-Ardenne* Namur – Burgundy, via Meuse, C des Ardennes, C de l'Aisne à la Marne, C latéral à la Marne, portion of C de la Marne au Rhin, C de la Marne à la Saône, Saône (Gray – St Jean-de-Losne)

10 *La Saône* Corre – Lyon

11 *Canal du Midi* Atlantic – Mediterranean, including C du Rhône à Sète and Petit Rhône

12 *Brittany* Rance C d'Ille et Rance, Vilaine, C de Nantes à Brest, Erdre

13 *Pays de la Loire* Sarthe, Mayenne, Oudon, Maine and Loire (upstream to Angers), C de Nantes à Brest (Nantes – Redon)

14 *Nord Pas-de-Calais* Liaison à Grande Gabarit (Dunkerque – Valenciennes), C de Lens, Deule, C de Roubaix, C de Furnes, C de Bergues, C de Bourbourg, Aa, C de Calais, Lys, Scarpe, C du Nord (northern part)

16 *Le Rhône* Lyon – Mediterranean, Petit Rhône, C d'Arles à Fos

17 *Canal de la Marne au Rhin* Vitry-le-François – Strasbourg, C des Houillères de la Sarre, C du Rhône au Rhin (Strasbourg – Rhinau)

18 *Bourgogne Waterways* Yonne, C de Bourgogne, C du Nivernais, Saône (St Jean-de-Losne – Chalon-sur-Saône).

24 *Picardie* C de la Somme, Liaison à Grand Gabarit (Arleux – Etrun), C du Nord, C de St Quentin, Sambre and C de la Sambre à l'Oise, C de l'oise à la'Aisne, Aisne and latéral canal, Oise and latéral canal.

25 *La Charente* Atlantic – Angoulème

26 *Canal de L'Est* Meuse Liège – Corre

27 *Le Lot* Luzech – St Cirq Lapopie

Carte Guide du Doubs et Canal du Rhône au Rhin Vagnon No 2 Les Éditions du Plaisancier, Caluire, France Saône – Rhine.

Le Rhin et la Moselle Éditions de la Navigation du Rhin, Strasbourg. Massive ring-bound chart book, covering Rhine (Switzerland to

North Sea), Moselle (Rhine – Neuves-Maisons) and German Sarre.
Enterprise Guides, Enterprise Publications, Bideford, Devon.
(English text. Especially useful for shopping/tourism/history with
detailed restaurant recommendations.)
1 *Canal du Midi and Canal du Rhône à Sète* 1991
2 *The Yonne and the Nivernais* 1992
3 *The Canal de Bourgogne* 1990
4 *The Charente* 1992

Travelogues

Watersteps Through France, Bill and Laurel Cooper, Mandarin
paperback, 1992. (The Somme to the Camargue by Dutch barge.)
Travels with 'Lionel' Hart, Massey, Gollanz, 1988 (OP). (Travels by
small barge.)
Slow Boat Through France, Hugh McKnight, distributed by
Shepperton Swan, 1991. (Cruisers of TSDY *Avonbay* over many of
the most attractive routes.)
Small Boat Series, Roger Pilkington, Macmillan. All OP, but often
available through Shepperton Swan Ltd, The Clock House, Upper
Halliford, Shepperton, Middlesex TW17 8RU (Tel 0932 783319).
Titles include *Alsace*, 1961; *France*, 1964; *Southern France*, 1965;
Meuse, 1967; *Luxembourg*, 1967; *Midi* (Pearson, Burton-on-Trent),
1989.

Index

OTHER TITLES AVAILABLE FROM ADLARD COLES NAUTICAL

All these books are available or can be ordered from your local bookshop or can be ordered direct from the publisher. Simply tick the titles you want and fill in the form below.

Prices and availability subject to change without notice

Adlard Coles Nautical Cash Sales, PO Box 11, Falmouth,
Cornwall. TR10 9EN

Please send a cheque or postal order for the value of the book and add the following for postage and packing.

UK including BFPO: £1.00 for one book plus 50p for the second book and 30p for each additional book ordered up to a £3.00 maximum.

OVERSEAS INCLUDING EIRE: £2.00 for the first book, plus £1.00 for the second book, and 50p for each additional book ordered.

OR Please debit this amount from my Access/Visa Card (delete as appropriate).

Card number

Amount £ . . . .

Expiry date . . . .

Signed . . . .

Name . . . .

Address . . . .

Fax no: 0326 376423 . . . .